The Kids Are the Easy Part

An Insider's Perspective on School Reform

The Kids Are the Easy Part

An Insider's Perspective on School Reform

Benedict A. Baglio

McKenna Publishing Group
Indian Wells, California

The Kids Are The Easy Part-An Insider's Perspective on School Reform

ISBN: 1-932172-23-8
LCCN: 2005936070

Cover design by Leslie Parker

First Edition
10 9 8 7 6 5 4 3 2 1
Printed in the United States of America

Visit us on the Web at: www.mckennapubgrp.com

If the misery of our poor be caused
not by the laws of nature,
but by our institutions, great is our sin.

—C. Darwin, *Voyage of the Beagle*

Table of Contents

Forward

I started writing this on my first official day of retirement, July 27, 2004, although the words began to morph in September of 1968, when I entered the eighth grade homeroom I was assigned in Sagamore Junior High School on Long Island to begin my career in education. Heretofore I was confident and steadfast as to my purpose and my abilities, but when I picked up the attendance roster to perform the age-old tradition of calling the first-day-of-school roll, I found my mouth dry and my hands shaking. Welcome to the jungle...

I'd rather write historical fiction. The research for my first published novel, *A String of Pearls,* was a labor of love and great fun to write. At first, I wanted to write this book as a sort of Catch-22 of education, lampooning individuals I had come to know in my career and the absurdity of the system that ruled us. My publisher, Eric Bollinger, advised me otherwise. Conversations we had the previous summer, my recent award of the doctorate in education, and my affection for our young and our best educators (I miss them already), convinced me that the subject of education and its reform were much too important to treat flippantly. My career, as I think of it, was also a labor of love. However, when I think of the systemic absurdity that marked a good part of it, the truth is not all that far removed from the fiction I take great pleasure in writing. You can't make this stuff up.

You may ask why I didn't write this sooner. Well, I think you have to be at the end of the trail to reflect back on what it was like without reservations or compromises on original thought. Hindsight is 20/20, but one can be awfully myopic in discussing the present, and necessarily cautious about the unknowns of the future. My present is done; all I have is the past, as I won't be going to work tomorrow.

What this book seeks to do is to provide the reader, be you an educational professional, parent, student, board of education member, politician, or interested bystander, a look through my eyes at the process and system we call education from an insider's perspective that was developed over the span of a thirty-six-year career, and my ideas of what real school reform should encompass. It is not pure research in any sense. It is not a work filled with data, though data is referenced. It is not replete with educational jargon that would cloud its message, but uses it to identify and explain process. It refers to research done forty or more years ago as well as articles from professional journals and newspapers that I read as I completed this text. A good deal of what I say was said before, but I attempt to put it in the context of the new millennium. In any event, my hope is that you, the reader, will come to see that we are all victimized, uplifted, served, abused, flimflammed, and sometimes encouraged by forays against an anachronistic systems and processes that confound us while trying to empower us. More than anything, I hope that you come to see that there can be better, much more cost-effective ways to make education more responsive, universal, attainable, equitable, people-friendly, and more in line with making it worthy of those who come seeking it. Shouldn't we expect more than just standards-based competency? If not that, shouldn't every student at least be a competent and functioning and learning human being?

I thought for a very brief, fleeting moment to entitle this book Educational Reform for Dummies, but there are so many books out there using the "dummy" expression, and, like I mentioned, I didn't want to appear flippant. I don't know about you, but every time I see a title that encapsulates the phrase "for Dummies," I feel a little more inadequate about what I don't know. I also thought that many of you would have made a quick leap of logic to think that the title would suggest oxymoron. I want to impress upon you here and now that education should really be about choice and pursuing our interests, not about being dumb concerning what we don't know or have no interest in. Yet, that's how we run our system and how we measure our kids. There is more untapped and wasted genius out there caused by the system than developed by it. If we are dummies at all, it is because we have let the system push us around to the point that our thinking is more concerned about what we don't know and aren't good at, as opposed to what we do know and are interested in, and how we can learn more about it. We all need to work a lot harder at developing our skills—much harder. We do this by challenging our weaknesses, not being buried by them. The memorable genius Stephen J. Gould wrote an incredibly insightful book called *The Mismeasure of Man* that speaks of how through the ages we have been spending more time on what people cannot do and classifying them for it, rather than making the best of the gifts, talents, and interests we have. We have been so interested in quantifying and labeling things that it limits our asking questions about what we do not know or cannot measure. He quotes John Stuart Mill:

The tendency has been so strong to believe that whatever received a name must be an entity or being, having an independent existence of its own. And if no real entity answering to the name could be found, men did not for that reason suppose that none existed, but imagined that it was something peculiarly abstruse and mysterious (p. 320).

A caveat: this book offers a glimpse of my view of systemic reform. Metaphorically speaking, it is not a buffet menu, but a complete dinner with no substitutions. That means that one cannot cite part of it as the key to "fix" the system because a specific theme strikes congruency to an individual's particular position or politics, while the rest can be ignored. Take all of it into account, or none of it. As in a fine restaurant, there is no substituting rice for potatoes. If you disagree with any of it, that makes room for informed discourse, or indeed may prompt you, the reader, to write his or her own book. Taking one idea out of context is compromising the whole of it. The problems indeed go far beyond the schoolhouse door and cannot be engaged piecemeal. My career has been marked by incidences of cognitive dissonance, vacuous idealism, and rampant catch-phrase driven opportunism. Please, don't do this to my book.

I also ask the reader to remember that change is a constant. If schools do not change, they will be changed. This book contains examples of the effects of change when it comes from an external force, and not part of a constant internal reflectiveness that promotes and demands organizational change.

I have no particular axe to grind, though you might have already concluded that I do. I accomplished much, and I had a wonderful career with the privilege of working with some super teachers, fine community members, and a few generations of fantastic kids. I was a part of their triumphs, tragedies and a few of their deaths... too many deaths. However, I hope this book makes you a critical participant rather than a casual observer of educational process, to the point that you pay very close attention to what your state and federal legislators do, to what your local boards of education and teachers' unions do, and most of all, what we do to our children

14

with poorly informed inquiry and too much groundless political passion and special interest, and yet with the best of intentions (and you know where that paving leads). You also need to know there is no one to particularly single out and blame. That's being ridiculous. We have all obviated our responsibilities as educational institutions, parents, and as a society by relying on labels rather than action, and modeling programs after others that have not worked. I'll discuss how and why, and give you some ideas on which to ruminate and masticate (SAT words).

We are all much better than the educational system we so blindingly and obediently support with our money and careers. And, the kids deserve better. As Americans, we deserve the absolute best. Nobody in the world works harder than we do, though we are bullied and lied to into thinking that we are all lazy and inept. It's politically expedient for those in power to find an "enemy out there" rather than take the blame for the shortcomings that plague us. We elect them to change things, yet they become consumed with the status quo. I found it quite odd that the governor of Arkansas attacked the nation's high schools as being devoid of rigor, but heavy on rigor mortis. Then I realized that if anyone would be able to identify rigor mortis, it would be a politician who regularly thrives on it. They show little leadership to stimulate and explain change to us. Yet when things go wrong, it's because we are lazy, greedy, inept, or unpatriotic in making the sacrifices to work harder, rather than working smarter. The tired labels of liberal, conservative, Republican, Democrat, right wing, left wing...whatever, are used to pin the blame on some political philosophy that is long dead, but still breathes life into lost causes because it's the easy thing to do. It's becoming incredibly boring, as well as an incredibly inefficient way to do business. Perhaps we need to invent a label termed Expediter...you know, someone who gets things done by talking to the American people, who to my mind show a goodness and strength under fire like no other people in history.

Change needs to be dramatic. The time for tinkering is long gone—as I think of it, it probably left with the Edsel or when Sputnik blasted aloft from Balkanor Space City in the 1950's. Changes in the national culture and on the international stage were not met with commensurate changes in how we enculture and educate our kids. We have let golden opportunities flash past as we stringently stayed the course in the anachronistic, selective, and discriminatory systems and structures we use in engaging our youngsters. Worse, we depersonalized education, and made it an obsolescent, industrial age factory still plagued with an agrarian age calendar.

There is a joke of sorts that envisions that a doctor, engineer, a soldier, and a teacher who died 100 years ago are miraculously brought back from the dead for a glimpse at how their respective occupational fields have changed. The doctor would be amazed at the modern operating room, the development of wonder drugs, and instruments that peer painlessly into the human body. The engineer would marvel at the Boeing 777, modern automobiles, and new alloys and materials used to build our modern world. Even the technology surrounding the ubiquitous compact disc would provide hours of wonder. The soldier would be aghast at how technical and lethal war has become, from the weapons of the infantryman to the Stealth B-2 bomber. The teacher, on the other hand would walk into his or her traditional workplace, see the familiar twenty-five seats arranged in rows of five down and five across, and the trusty chalkboard equipped with the most modern eraser and dustless chalk. With a day or two to review the text, he or she could begin the process of teaching, expecting to end the day at 3:00 p.m., and end the year sometime around June 1, plus or minus a few weeks depending on the school's locale. In fact, there's a chance that the teacher might very well be teaching in the exact same school that he or she taught in the first time around—the same poorly heated, un-air conditioned facility, with lots of steps to go from floor to floor, even for the kids who struggle with legs or arms that don't work. Those kids didn't go to school back then, so the steps weren't a problem. To be sure, the computer would present itself as a new-fangled device, but its use might well be limited to doing the same 100 year-old rote tasks albeit with futuristic bells and whistles. More than not, the teacher would be somewhat shocked, or perhaps pleased, that his or her preactice was narrowed to preparing students for an endless stream of mandated high stakes testing, while his engineering, medical, and military contemporaries had immersed themselves in sifting through the cutting edge technologies and methodologies, and the modern systems and new structures and possibilities they fostered.

The teacher would also notice that while the tools and temporality of the school year haven't changed all that much, the color of the classroom has. There are Asian faces, African American faces, and Hispanic faces, as well as faces that cannot be readily categorized to accompany the familiar white faces. If the teacher were a high school teacher, he or she might note that many of his or her charges cannot speak or write English, or read or write in their own native language, yet they attend every day. Those students simply weren't around the high school 100 years ago. Anyone who finished grade eight back then was considered pretty clever. In this vein, the high school teacher would also note with some degree of amazement that half the enrollment in the high school class consisted of young women. Half of any grade level roster would represent children from single-parent families. Lastly, the teacher would be surprised at the political power the profession now yields.

If the school could be metaphorically compared to a house, its kitchen, the center of creativity that feeds the process of inquiry, would be cooking with coal, the living room would be heated in the same manner, and the bedrooms, those dens of reflection and dreams, would remain cold at night. The rigid, tired structure of the house defies attempts to enlarge and modernize it. For example, the dining room cannot possibly house and feed the complement of diverse humanity that now comes to dinner. The house's dimensions in the contexts of time and space confound the reformer with their relatively limited experiential possibilities and expectations, stubbornly serving eras and populations that had long since changed in scope and sequence. While the house was landscaped, painted, and wallpapered to appear freshened, its intrinsic structure remains stubbornly frozen, despite the fact that through the years it became too small, then too big, too antiquated, too much ignored, and prone to handyman quick fixes to repair it to address the changing times and the new varieties of families it was built to serve with the best of 100-year-old intentions. The yellow buses in the driveway obscure the house's windows, and at the same time limit access and deny possibilities. Perhaps rather than constantly patching it, it would be more cost and people effective to tear it down. The building may represent what some may refer to as proud traditions, that changing them only means a regression of expectations. To this, I counter that it past time that those proud traditions find new expressions.

I once heard the Honorable Stephen Sanders of the New York State Assembly remark that he wanted new schools in his assembly district, as some of them were pre-war schools. When countered that schools built prior to World War II were still sound and proper, he responded, "Not World War II...the Spanish-American War!" I do not think he was talking solely about the edifices.

The book is divided into chapters by topic, so as to make the reader familiar with specific problems and strengths of the present educational paradigm. However, it is important to remember that each of these topics is not a stand-alone, individualized entity. All are related and interdependent.

Lastly, don't take offense if you are a member of a group that is discussed in a context of needed change. It is not about you, but about creating a system of education in which we can all be proud and flourish, especially the kids. Like I said, we are all better than what we have wrought, and giving a bit will mean gaining much. I'm not utopian, to be sure. Clearly, one thing I have learned in the past thirty-six years is that we are noble people pursuing a noble cause who have somehow chosen the wrong vehicle and took a few wrong turns on our crusade to educate our young. The task will become increasingly harder unless we step back, create a new map, buy a new car, and take a new perspective. Herein is mine.

Benedict A. Baglio, Ed.D.
July 27, 2004

Chapter 1
So, Where Do We Start?

I think a good place to begin would be for me to make some axiomatic assumptions, some based on my experiences, others taken from the current literature regarding school reform.

Children's perceptions of the world around them are formed practically from birth. In line with this;

Parents are the children's first and most influential teachers. The responsibility is enormous, and the art of parenting becomes more difficult with each generation. Too many parents are obviating their responsibilities. Some do it willingly; others because they have little choice, still others because of systemic indifference to society's needs.

The word "parent" is a noun and a verb. It therefore signifies a title as well as action. There is nothing that sounds dumber than an outraged parent who shows up the last few days of school and claims he or she didn't know his or her child was failing. There is a flood of correspondence that comes home to keep parents informed about the school's activities, and their child particularly. If it didn't get there, either your mailman is co-opting your mail (hardly) or your child is taking it (probably). Don't you think it would be time to call the school after twenty weeks goes by and no correspondence is received as to how the child was doing?

Kids are much more aware today because events are "real time." The media is everywhere, and as a result, so are more immediate choices. Communication between parent and child is more important now than ever before, but the pace of the world in which we live condenses the time to be effective at it. Worse, the U.S. worker puts in more time than any other in the world, so the amount of family time at home is at an all-time low. To add to this paradox, for one of every two families, the capacity to communicate has been halved, as one parent is absent. Kids are forced to make major decisions every day just to survive, but this is not recognized or appreciated by the school as a legitimate part of learning. This is a major problem, and needs to be directly addressed. Parental participation cannot be hinted at as being a good thing, nor can the parental role be patronized. All parents must (let me emphasize must) be unequivocally active participants.

The overwhelming majority of kids will do what you ask them to do, as long as they perceive it as fair and in their interests. They are mostly eager educational participants, and are keenly perceptive. They can discern true interest in their welfare as opposed to forcing them into systemic compliance. They do not suffer fools easily, nor are they unaware of the immediate world around them. They are much more aware than we care to admit, or are unwise enough not to.

Kids are a long-term project. They are in the public schools for 13 years. There are no quick fixes, nor miracle programs to produce learners. Tests will never show what kids really know or what they can really do. They are limited and incomplete assessments. While kids may dress the same, use the same idiomatic expressions, and share the youth culture "du jour," they are unique as individuals. Each has a talent, each a weakness. What works for one may be anathema to another. It would be good to remember that kids are the only ones in the school who are not paid to be there, and though they are recognized as the target of reform efforts, they do not recognize this role—they don't have any voice in any educational policy originating at the local, state, or national level.

When kids leave the elementary school to go to middle or junior high school, and then on to the high school, their transitions are not akin to them leaving the planet or the current dimension. Schools are structured as if the child disappears upon reaching the "next level." Continuity and responsibility are a specific problem for schools and kids.

Change in schools is traditionally conducted by incorporating the change agent within the rigid structures and systems of the school. Therefore, current reform efforts fall short of their mark, as reform is already compromised at the school's door. This would include standards-based instruction and high stakes tests. It is mistakenly referred to at times as "reform on the cheap." It is not true reform and it certainly is not cheap.

Reform efforts directed at the student as the problem, not the system, become cyclic in reintroducing previously ineffective efforts through a process the organizational theorist Peter Senge termed intensification; that is, if it doesn't work at first, try a bigger hammer. Others refer to it as insanity; that is, doing the same thing over again under a different title, and being just as disappointed when it doesn't work. For reform to work, the structures and systems of the school must be renewed or replaced.

Unless a school's capacity is changed along with its rigid structures and systems, reform will fail. Reform done on the cheap is not cheap in the long term, nor is it effective in the short term. Mostly, it ends up merely propping up failing structure.

As a corollary to this;

Education is not cheap, but much less expensive in the larger sense as a tool to change failed social policy. Crime, dependency on welfare, health care, domestic abuse, and drug and alcohol abuse vary inversely with educational achievement. We need to move to a preventional educational model that will be more expensive in the short term, but much less expensive in the long term, in human and monetary terms, than the interventional model in use.

Copying foreign educational models will not work. From our start at Philadelphia's Independence Hall in 1776, at least on paper, we declared ourselves unique as a nation—heterogeneous, righteous, brave, entrepreneurial, deliberative, intuitive, reflective, indefatigable, bright, fair-minded, altruistic, and centered on the individual.

Why we would even contemplate copying what a foreign nation does in educating its kids? This is not to say we are doing a great job educating our kids...we are not. It is to say that we don't need to embrace a foreign model that is used to educate a specific homogenous population to fix our system. We do a bad enough job of it ourselves and we live here. Note, though, the rest of the world is using education as the new super weapon. The computer-related jobs we are outsourcing to India and China were once considered the sole propriety of the United States. When I had a problem with my new Dell computer, the person who helped me fix it over the "800" phone line was Gary, a pleasant chap who lives in New Delhi.

In line with this;

There is no such thing as specific occupational training as a goal of education, because specific training will continue to produce workers for jobs that have been eliminated or have not as yet been invented. Broad curricula partly based on technology as businesses see it, experientially delivered with a strong, directly related foundation in the liberal arts would better serve the student. Two programs, Technical Preparation ("Tech Prep") and School-to-Careers, both federally sponsored, were headed in this direction. Unfortunately, each was pummeled into extinction by the questionable demands of the No Child Left Behind legislation and a termination of their funding.

We are the only superpower left in the world and have historically accomplished the impossible almost routinely. For example, there are the flags of only two nations on the moon. The Soviet flag was put there by a robot. The American flag was planted on lunar soil by American moonwalkers—five times. (Though its flag never got there, Apollo 13 was an exercise in the doing the impossible as well). The flag placed there by the Soviet robot represents a totalitarian nation that doesn't exist any more, thanks to us. American education, uneven as it is, made all this ingenuity possible.

In many schools, discipline has taken a pre-eminent role over instruction, completely the inverse of its purpose. Among other systemic issues, it is failing instructional methodologies, stale and irrelevant curricula, school size, narrow leadership, inadequate teacher preparation, and poor staff development practices that lead to discipline problems. Good discipline, whatever that means in a particular locale, does not mean anybody is learning. Schools with "good discipline" may have high dropout rates, high suspension rates, low daily attendance, and a cultural disconnect between the school and a good part of the student body. Disaffected kids who are not there, physically or mentally, cannot learn. Schools not actively supported by parents cannot teach or learn. Security guards are not teachers and metal detectors are not instructional implements.

The farther away the center of reform is from the student, the less its meaning. Congress, state houses, and educational agencies cannot dictate policy unilaterally with any hope of achieving success.

Educational leadership is incredibly important, yet it is not something we define, covet, and nurture in our teachers or administrators.

Just because you went to school doesn't make you an expert on how schools should be. I don't say this condescendingly (okay, a little condescendingly), but your participation as a student gave you only an inkling of only what was wrong, not how it got that way. Your experiences matched with an open-minded historical and operational perspective, however, can give you a clearer insight into schools as they are today.

Much is made of the No Child Left Behind provision for school choice. School choice is admittance that there are inequalities and inequities among schools. Having kids transfer to "good schools" or "charter schools" won't fix the problems for the kids who choose or are forced to stay in a failing school. As a result, lots of kids are being left behind with the best of intentions.

Education can be fixed, all of it, but it will need a major overhaul. What is in place right now is absurdly out of date and out of touch with the present as well as the future. It didn't work much better forty or fifty years ago, either

Education is the most important thing we as a nation do. Mind you, I said do. It is not a product, but a lifelong process. It will ultimately decide our fate in a world of countries that are educating more and more of their populations. Education must be broad-based in concept, as the world for which we educate a current kindergartner will be radically different than the one he or she will inherit as a college graduate.

The overwhelming majority of people working in the educational field are working hard. Their day begins early on and, contrary to popular opinion, does not end when the kids leave the building. Required graduate study, reviewing student work, extra help, meetings, parent conferences, extracurricular activities, and a variety of other obligations keep us there well after the kids leave (oh, I have known my share of clock-punchers. The system protects them, and this is a tragedy, as they demean the rest of us). This is true at every level of education, from elementary school to graduate school. While we work hard, we are not working smart, as we bind our activities to the traditional school day and school year, two anachronistic structures that need revision, and attach ourselves to other systems that are determined to enforce the status quo.

Schools are not as good as they used to be. I don't know if they ever were. Except for a very few courses (Miss Supernaw, I still fondly remember you!) and activities, I did not particularly see my public school years as formative as they could have been, and as a first-year teacher I had visions of making grand changes for my charges. Yet the system persists as I found it thirty-six great (but consistently frustrating) years ago. I have had students who graduated ten or fifteen years ago return to the schools in which I practiced and said the place had really changed, and the kids were really crazy. Funny thing, but I saw none of that. I think memories play tricks on those of us who do not seriously reflect on our experiences. We fondly remember the great times while we put the bad memories aside. Regrettably, many with fond memories have blamed too much of their failure on themselves, not the institution.

School should not be about this. It all should be positive and memorable as an opportunity to build confidence, respect for others, competency, resiliency, and an understanding that learning is an intuitive and complicated, but not nearly impossible, lifelong process. Learning should encompass tutelage in democracy and the criticality democracy demands if it is to survive. School should be the first to teach us that we get by and get ahead with the social construction of solutions to difficult problems, that no one gives us tests to determine if we are successful citizens, husbands, wives, fathers, mothers, and grandparents. It should be a time that champions great failure, for it is in failure that we learn the best lessons, and how not to fail again. I'm not talking about failure of the sort that the system assesses through exams, but the kind that results from the experiential experimentation in the company of teachers and fellow students. The Wright Brothers almost killed themselves learning to fly, and Columbus never made it to India. That is not the kind of failure that gets you sent to summer school for six weeks to "learn" at least sixty-five percent of the work (what about the thirty-five percent you don't learn—is it not important?) so the system can wash its hands in a seemingly altruistic basin that is actually its way of displacing its systemic shortcomings on the student.

The educational system requires a contextual world-view. If the world is a smaller place because of mass media, we ought to make every effort to meet the new neighbors.

Not every one should go to college, but everyone should have the educational experiences to make an informed choice. In this vein, community colleges are the most undervalued of all our educational institutions. They complete connections, correct misconnections, and center on the student, not a specific program or strand of research, as the basis for educational continuity. And, they are bargains. I am going to discuss all of the above in the coming chapters.

Chapter 2
American Kids, American Schools, and Tragedy—September 11-12, 2001

This one comes from the heart. September 11-12, 2001 had more of a profound effect on me than I had originally thought. I share this with you to give my take of what kids are really all about, beyond the clothes, the piercings, and the media images. I also relate this to the purpose of schooling as I have come to hope it might be.

September 11, 2001 will live in my memory as a catastrophic event only second to the assassination of President John F. Kennedy. To Sammy Stahlman, in his late seventies, an accomplished businessman, former board of education member, community leader, and now a substitute teacher and honorary football coach, a veteran of Utah Beach on D-Day, and one of my dear friends, longevity allowed him to add the attack on Pearl Harbor to this historical context of national tragedy. Personally, the horror of the day was marked by the death of Sammy's only son, murdered by al-Qaeda as he worked in Tower One at the stock firm of Cantor-Fitzgerald.

I was involved in getting materials together to speak to a class of seniors about the final stages of the college admissions process when my son called me from his Boston office to ask if I had known that a plane had just crashed into one of the twin towers of the World Trade Center. I tuned the radio to one of the local FM stations and heard a confused but calm announcer describe what he knew about the incident. Another song played, but then the music abruptly ended. The announcer's voice lost its merriment as he interviewed somebody on the scene to describe the disaster. The onlooker described in complete horror that a plane now had hit the second tower, and both buildings were burning.

25

One of the counselors with whom I worked was wracked with concern, as her long-time boyfriend worked in the Towers as a trader for Cantor-Fitzgerald. It turned out that he was among the missing (his remains were identified months later). Her students were comforting, as all this happened so quickly that the normalcy of the day had intertwined with the tragedy of the moment. Then one of our business education teachers came to the office to report that one of the towers had collapsed.

New York City is only fifty miles away from the district in which I practiced. I knew we would have other members of our community who had relatives, friends, or significant others who were working in the city that day. Two of our high school students lost fathers who were firefighters trapped when the towers collapsed. The other kids somehow knew this and gravitated to them to provide comfort.

Parents came to the high school to bring their kids home, not so much that they sensed an imminent danger, but because they simply wanted to be with their kids. One father, a recent immigrant who spoke broken English, wept that his father had told him just before he recently died that the world his kids would inherit would be a much more dangerous place than his world. When we couldn't immediately find his child, he became anxious and cried on my shoulder. I tried to reassure him that everything would be all right, that there was just a minor mix-up, and his daughter would be down to the office in a moment. She was.

I tried to present a sense of calm. One of the other counselors suggested that this had to be the worst time in our history. I countered that World War II was more the danger to our way of life in my relatively limited opinion, as whole nations had turned their armies to wreak fascist terror. I was trying to give her an historical perspective, as well as to give my racing mind something to grind on—my own son worked in mid-town New York City, as did a nephew (both were mentally shaken, but physically fine).

The kids remained calm. One young lady castigated her mother for coming to take her home, that she was in the middle of a test, and telling her not to panic. "We're Americans, for God's sake!" she yelped. A few members of the football team reacted by saying that practice today (it was canceled) would be particularly physical, as if to give a message of defiance to the miscreants that murdered their fellows. Other kids sought the counsel of their teachers to ask questions, talk, or just listen. The kids did not panic. They just wanted to know...

One of the responsibilities of administrators in this particular district that were not assigned directly to a school building was to cover for elementary building principals in their absence. As it turned out, one my good friends, a principal whose absences for illness over the span of his thirty plus—year career could be counted on his fingers, had a minor medical procedure that was a long time in scheduling and couldn't be missed. Thus, on September 12, after a restless night spent reminiscing about our tenth wedding anniversary celebrated at the Trade Center's rooftop restaurant "Windows on The World," and a reception The College Board hosted barely a year past at that same place, followed by a pre-dawn run that was interrupted by my sobs at the sight of my neighbor's house draped with a spot-lit American flag, I reported to his elementary school to be principal for the day. I was confronted immediately by the chief custodian who informed me that an erstwhile patriot, in his or her zeal to lead the counterattack on al-Qaeda (probably from the foxhole in his or her living room), had cut the lanyards on the flagpole and made off with school's flag. I felt my blood boiling at the absolutely stupid insensitivity that perpetrated such an absurdly foolish act on this particular historical moment, but I had resolved after my early morning experience that my emotions would not get the best of me on this second day of days.

"I have another flag, but I have no way of running the lanyard up to the top of the pole through the ring to hoist it. Do you want to call the fire department? They might be able to send over a bucket truck to do it."

I hesitated. The first buses were pulling up to the building filled with children whom I'm sure would have rather been home with mommy and daddy today. What I didn't want was a fire truck that had been an icon of tragedy (it was too early in the crisis to have been transformed into an icon of heroism) to pull up to the building this beautiful fall morning. I didn't really know what was going on in the kids' heads. My answer to my chief custodian was shortly forthcoming. A second grader got off one of the first buses to pull up to the building and walked directly to me, eyeing the flagpole and me.

"Who are you?" he politely asked. "Is Mr. V here?"

"I'm Mr. Baglio. I'm here because Mr. V is sick today. And who might you be?"

"I'm Rick. Where's the flag?" he said, pointing to the empty apex of the flagpole, somewhat in a demanding voice but tinted with more concern than confrontation. Other students I dubbed "Rick's posse," gathered around Rick as he spoke to me, all those little, beautiful faces with big eyes looking up to me.

"Someone stole it last night, Rick. I'm trying to figure out a way to get another one up..."

"We really need a flag today, Mr. Bag...Bagel...Bag-a-lio. It will kinda tell us everything is, um...you know...okay." He paused then looked at the empty flagpole. "When I say the Pledge, I look out at that flag because it's usually waving in the breeze. The one in the classroom doesn't look as nice."

So be it for the ruminations didactic to high-level administrative decisions. On the way inside the building to call the local fire department, a mother and her third grader were waiting for me. The little girl looked gray, her eyes lacking the shine that little kids use to melt us.

"She saw on TV what happened yesterday. We couldn't get her away from it last night," the mother said, "no matter what we tried. We didn't feel that being any sterner would help. Could you talk with her?"

"What's your name?" I asked, as kindly as one can ask such a question, kneeling to make eye contact on an even keel with the little girl.

"Jennifer," her voice squeaked.

"I'm Mr. Baglio."

"Hello," she said, taking my extended hand.

"So, what's troubling you?"

"I don't know. I'm just afraid...you know, about yesterday."

"So am I, Jennifer. But I needed to be here today, so I came."

"I need to be here, too, but I'm a little nervous. The buildings in the city..."

"Well, that is not going to happen here," I said as convincingly as I could. "I tell you what, Jen. Suppose you come down to check on me at lunchtime to see how I'm doing, and I'll check with you to see how you're doing?" Then, another thought. "You know, Jennifer, I'm going to be kind of busy today. Would you do me a favor? Maybe in the meantime, you can also check on how your teacher's doing, and how the rest of the class is doing. You can let me know at lunch."

"Okay," she said, a smile coming to her face. She hugged me. Jennifer had a mission.

The fire department obliged almost immediately, the volunteers bringing their huge bucket truck to the school within minutes of my call. I announced over the public address system that the students and teachers shouldn't be alarmed by the fire truck, that it was here on the specific mission to replace the flag an idiotic miscreant (I didn't say this to the children—I didn't have to as they knew only an idiotic miscreant would pull such a stunt) had taken the night before in the name of avenging America. I took Rick out of class to show him the flag.

"Ya know, Mr. Baglio, I think it has to come down halfway for awhile."

The chief custodian and I looked at each other in amazement. We forgot. Rick didn't. As we dropped the flag, Rick stood there like a little soldier and saluted it. Jennifer came down at lunch and told me her class talked about it, drew some pictures, she felt better, and that the class and her teacher were doing "okay." In fact, all the teachers were doing their absolute best "okay," and the kids were as well.

The flag-stealing miscreant should have witnessed what I was witness to in that elementary school that day and in the high school the day before if he or she wanted to know about patriotism and whipping the vaunted al-Qaeda. Courage under fire is the best way I can describe it, patriotism at its finest when parent, child, community, and educators came together to make sense and draw meaning from tragedy and do business as best as they could. While I had to be there, the kids did not, but they came or demanded to stay, overcoming their fears to share them with their peers, or show defiance in the face of terror, and to socially construct their thoughts on the bloodiest day in America's history. Their teachers, all of them, stood tall. There was no curriculum that day. The curriculum was what the kids brought to their classrooms, and their teachers became mentors and discussion leaders in sorting it all out and coming to a social construction of the events of the day.

One fellow administrator noted that when history sorts out the details of September 11, 2001, teachers and their schools will be credited for keeping the country together by providing a place for America's kids to dialogue, reflect, and study the events of the day, and consider how our lives would be forever changed. I know this happened after Kennedy's assassination while I was a senior in high school. Sammy tells me that it happened on Monday, December 8, 1941, when he knew that his life and the life of his close friends would soon be laid on the line for America, that mixed bag of culture, democratic values, dreams, and ideas we call home.

More than any other mission, this is what school is all about in a democracy. We tell the kids that by birthright they are endowed to be critical, yet schools today don't particularly provide this opportunity, to rely on a student's intentionality and experiences to interpret the academic means to the ends of criticality, to socially construct meaning from events and encounters. It doesn't happen as much as when disaster strikes.

Right in this historical moment, schools are consumed with test scores and narrowed curriculum designed to help students regurgitate discreet bits of knowledge on high stakes tests, which are not assessments of the broad brush of all there is to know as it happens and as it happened, so as to make a curricula more fluid and meaningful. Why? It's easier for the anachronistic structures

and systems of education, designed to prepare workers for an industrial age of repetitive, minimal thinking tasks to educate those
masses of students who never went past grade eight, to do it the
wrong way. It seems that only when we are challenged greatly do
we discard the ridiculous for the sublime, and take advantage of
the blessings of democracy that allow for dialogue and the critical
construction of meaning.

The late historian Stephen Ambrose, who served as the consultant for Steven Spielberg's *Saving Private Ryan* and Spielberg's
and Tom Hanks' *Band of Brothers,* two of the most definitive
historical accounts of World War II, commented that World War II
could ultimately be broken down into a battle bet ween the Boy
Scouts and The Hitler Youth. What does this mean? The Boys Scouts
are about self-motivated discovery, learning by experiencing, not
binding their learning with rigid frameworks or dogma. They are
about seizing the initiative and informed by teamwork for the
common good, and choosing among boundless opportunities.
They reference kindness, self-motivation, respect for everyone and
everything, and taking care of those who cannot make it on their
own. The Hitler Youth had been trained in hatred, racial superiority,
narrow dogma, the ultimacy of self, hatred for the weak, and blind
obedience. There was no reason to dialogue, only to obey. What was
written was supreme. Period. This vicious narrowness led to their
demise, because if you cannot think, you cannot improvise. A person denied their constructive being couldn't dialogue or question.
Truth is known only as judgment made by others, not learned by
constructed discovery in the company of others. The Boy Scouts
came home to create a superpower based on their early experiences that proved true in the crucible of war, and they didn't do
it by accepting limitations on their thinking or truth as someone
else defined it.

Why we choose to narrow what students learn in the name of
standards-based reform in turn narrows what students can define
as truth. It really is a poor method of exacting accountability from
schools, especially in a democracy. If test results are so high stakes
as to determine public shaming of schools in newspapers, the dismissal of principals and teachers, and the withholding of funds, you
know damn well that passing the test will become the educational
goal, no matter what the cost. The cost may include an end to recess, extra periods of rote drill, Saturday classes, the curtailment or
complete elimination of elective programs that kids covet, and the
purchase of specific test-prep related materials rather than primary
sources. In one Texas school, camouflaged test-prep materials were
distributed to students at an assembly conducted by a test-prep
group of dolts who were dressed in combat fatigues to "declare
war on the test!"

What is right and appropriate for one person to know may not be necessary or appropriate for everyone else. Experiential possibilities become stranded by the standards-based curricula geared to the passing of high stakes tests. This is not to say we should expect less, or that there are not certain skills we should expect all kids to know, or that testing is bad. Certainly in the 21st Century we should produce kids who can read and write proficiently in the context of their abilities and chosen paths, who can understand the rudiments of algebra and geometry, understand their heritage enough to dream to create a future worthy of our past, and know at least as much science as necessary to respect and protect the environment, understand the scientific relationships in their chosen occupational choices, the concepts of energy, to make informed decisions on the direction research should take, and the finite nature of the earth. More than anything, kids should also know they can change their minds, that it is never too late to go back to school to learn something new and different.

Before any of this can take place, however, we should insure that each child is provided the same access to knowledge, and that the schools we provide are equal in capacity. You cannot expect all children to learn when their schools, their teachers, and their communities are not up to the task. A high stakes test cannot equalize inadequate food and shelter, caring parents, crumbling schools, pre-natal care, pediatric health, narrowly trained teachers, or uncertified teachers. High stakes testing dogma would have you believe that this is not necessarily so, that passing the test will solve these problems, but that dismisses the argument before it begins. Learning for all children needs to start on an even playing field before the expectations can be set, and then those expectations should be incredibly high, not only for the kids, but everyone involved in their education. The New York Yankees, as dominant as they have been against their Boston Red Sox arch rivals thus far in the 2004 season (September proved differently), would never play all their games at Fenway, or with only eight men. Yet, we are asking poor kids to accept the edge the rich kids have and take the same tests. In fact, as I write this on August 5, 2004, New York's governor and state legislature have not settled on a state budget, meaning that school districts cannot set their budgets. This has been complicated by a New York State Supreme Court order to insure that every student is funded equally, as a result of a suit brought by a parent of a New York City child. While state budgets are traditionally late, this year's budget has set a new record for lateness. It also blatantly attests to the obviation of responsibility of elected officials to take care of the kids. That the courts got involved in this is a travesty. That the courts have been ignored is incredible. That politics have gone this far is unforgivable.

Should all kids share the same knowledge when each has a different interest? After elementary school, we should know what kids' strengths are and their weaknesses. Should we use middle school to confirm it, to give kids time to grow without the useless pressure of grades in curriculum that has little content, is repetitive, and changes from school to school within a school district, as well as out side of it? Should we use the same reading program (if I could find the magic formula to teach all children to read, I would be wealthy beyond my wildest dreams) when we know all kids are wired to read differently? Shouldn't curricula change as science, technology, and industry discover a new need? Should kids with an artist's gifts have to know the same amount of math as a kid who is ultimately headed for medical school? Conversely, should the kid whose talents would have us believe he or she is headed for medical school or a career in the sciences be held to the same standard for math as the kid whose talents appear to direct him or her to a career as a graphic artist? Shouldn't the depth of the math they learn be in direct line with their strengths? Should they all take the same tests? That would lead one to assume that the student taking AP Studio Art should take the same math as the student taking AP Physics (more on the AP program later). Isn't it more democratic to profit by minimizing a person's shortcomings and championing their strengths? Aren't a rigorous academic program, critically based thinking, and dialoguing better than a program based on rote memorization and test preparation? Most importantly, shouldn't kids have the opportunity to change their minds, and shouldn't the system be in compliant enough to allow for this? We all know of kids who "caught fire" at different ages.

As it stands, American kids are the most standards-based tested in the world—that includes their Japanese and German counterparts who we always hear so much about. Are they any better for it? I would say no, especially when I consider the work we really need to do, and the time and resources we are wasting.

Am I advocating a lowering of expectations of students? Absolutely and unequivocally no. In fact, I would increase demands in terms of time and the depth of their academic activity. However, I would include their voices to learn of their strengths and desires, and the voices of those who will ultimately educate those students in the jobs they take and the colleges and technical schools they choose to attend after leaving the K-12 environment in their journey as lifelong learners. This way, the standards are realistic and aimed directly to the benefit of the student, and their assessments follow suit—and they change with the times, in a structure and system that allows for change in curriculum and the desires of the kids. The question of how this might occur is addressed in the forthcoming chapters.

Before you assume otherwise, I think there are common threads of knowledge all kids need to know, and that testing is necessary. The frequency, nature, and the outcomes of this testing, though, need to be really well defined. We may know that a student may be deficient in English or math after fourth grade testing. Besides giving the student "remediation," which consists of more frequent test-item centered drill (Senge's concept of intensification, which usually means a student is taken from an elective course he or she may enjoy that highlights their strengths, or worse, recess), we need to reassess our teaching and the context in which it occurs, and the student's ability to learn in greater depth.

By the way, I visited that class of seniors I was planning for on September 11 a few days afterwards to talk about college. The kids were kind of sluggish, not ready to talk about the future when the present seemed so rife with sadness. I started my talk with them by saying, "If your future plans have changed as a result of September 11, the bad guys won."

Faces stared up from their books; eyebrows were raised. Some smiled, some were resolute. The questions regarding college started coming. Someone had to give permission to the kids to look ahead. That was all they needed. It was something educators needed to do, and did across the country. What we need to do now is remember that those kids showed up. They learned and knew democracy's lessons and expectations full well by experiencing it, and they relied on each other and us. You can't standardize this action, nor can you assess it with a test. Yet, it was probably the most important day in education's history since World War II.

Chapter 3
Standards and High Stakes Assessments—
How Did We Get To This Place?

The following quote is attributed to Andrew Draper in 1906, the first commissioner of education in New York State under Governor Theodore Roosevelt, but his words will likely seem familiar to the contemporary observer of educational policy and practices:

...the state does not say that any school must follow the syllabus or take these examinations. It does not distribute money on the basis of success in the examinations. It does say that any school, which claims the state's money, must submit to the state's tests. And it does say that the higher educational standards and requirements for which it assumes responsibility must be completely met in some definite and exact manner for which it is able to vouch... if there are any people in New York who possess a school which they think ought not to have any exact standards or respond to any known tests, and if they will relinquish their claim upon the state's moneys, we will have to let them go their own sweet way until their experiences bring them to their senses.

A dissertation written a few years back by Chris Mazzeo at Stanford University indicated that there is a pathology to the dialectic regarding the national fervor to hold education accountable through the policy lever of standards-based curriculum measured by high stakes assessment, and like its predecessors this current reform has not been without controversy surrounding the ends and the essence of the educational experience for children—are state standards and their accompanying assessments a path to equity, accountability, and restructuring, or will they perpetuate current practice, foster greater inequity, and narrow curriculum to deny the motivations of those being educated? Are students to be viewed as quantified objects of state-sponsored assessment, or self-motivated learners? Will an emphasis on measurement and accountability result in people who are thinkers, immersed in the nation's cultural and political life, or narrowed beings that are solely "spending money" in the context of human capital?

How did this present educational reform get to this standards-and-assessments place and time? Kieran Egan in the November 2003 issue of *Educational Leadership* indicated that Horace Mann gave the first standardized written essay test in Massachusetts to replace the traditional oral examination in 1845. Way back in the 15th century in Treviso, Italy, teacher salaries were linked to student examination performance. Going back this far can help explain our history of testing, but I think my purpose would be better served by putting our historical context within a generation or so. Thus, as with any story there needs to be a beginning, and the beginning of standards-based reform I choose to use as a jumping off point can be traced to the 1983 U.S. Department of Education's report A Nation At Risk: The Imperative of Educational Reform. It was an impassioned plea for educational reform as a vehicle to address the nation's economic doldrums and social ills of the post-Vietnam era. Its language was direct and curt, dichotomously seeking to place blame, but at the same time praising education's accomplishments. For example, it argued that the educational system was so terrible that it would be an act of war if it were imposed by an unfriendly foreign power, squandering the gains in student achievement made in the wake of the Sputnik challenge; it also stated that urban areas recently reported gains in elementary student achievement, and more high schools offered advanced placement programs, and reported record numbers of graduates. A Gallup poll taken in 1983 indicated that eighty-seven percent of those familiar with A Nation At Risk supported its recommendations and that seventy-five percent of the public at-large favored testing that would determine promotion. The report aimed the dialectic about the purported educational misfortunes of children, but not to children about their educational misfortunes.

Reactions were predictable, depending on what side of the argument one supported. Some construed the report as a relatively low-risk venture of creating a politicized curriculum, as arguing for an educational system that is stringently accountable has always been in fashion. Society's reliance on technology begs the question: are our high school students doing as well in science and math as Japanese and German students? During the Cold War, we asked the same question of students in the Soviet Union and China. The enemy is always "out there." It was as if those seniors of the Class of 1983 were being blamed for the egregious state of our Union, those same seniors born in 1966 as the bloodiest phase of the deeply divisive Vietnam War was beginning, in the heart of the Civil Rights Movement that caused us to reappraise our values, to accompany one of the greatest eras of social change in the nation's short history that climaxed with Watergate. Failed foreign policy, myopic business and economic practices, government scandal, and social injustices were not the problem—it was the kids, who weren't old enough to vote, and their schools.

The unbroken line of standards-and-assessment based political rhetoric spanned six presidential terms culminating with the Clinton Administration's enactment of the Goals 2000 in 1994, which provided dollars for the states to draft educational standards and tests. By 1996, nearly every state was attempting to align standards and assessments, determining how to use test scores, and how to add resources to the system.

The Goals 2000 legislation set the blueprint for standards-based reform. Content standards (curriculum) were to outline the concepts and skills students should know at each level of their schooling to help school districts make judgments about curriculum. Performance standards (assessments), would indicate the level of performance students should demonstrate and were set to help them determine how good is good enough. Opportunity to Learn (OTL) standards were meant to guarantee all students would have adequate opportunity, in the form of finance and equity-related issues, to meet both content and performance standards. This implied that school structures and systems would be funded to induce systemic change (smaller class sizes, professional development for teachers, updated equipment and adequate supplies, different scheduling patterns) in low performing schools with little capacity to improve.

Those who advocated for standards-based reform and assessment as a policy lever for improving schools and student learning predicted that, through standards-based reform, education had the capacity to engage this historic moment with a triple-front attack:

That data generated by standards-based reform and assessment would focus attention on the issues of equity and accountability.

To establish a national commitment to education heretofore non-existent.

To improve the educational lot of poor children and children of color.

It is argued that hard data produced by tests, whether they are viewed as evil or enlightened, would demonstrate that what was a matter of philosophical debate has essentially been defined literally in black and white terms, that poor kids and kids of color are being marginalized by sub-standard instruction, facilities, and faculties, and all of this must end, and end now. Now that the rules of academic enterprise were defined publicly, the vital OTL standards would address historical inequities, missteps, and errant policies that have governed the structure and systems schools.

Unfortunately, the OTL Standards as a mandate to states wishing to qualify for federal dollars were eliminated from the legislation in an amendment passed in April 1996. This action paved the way to measure the success of standards-based reform by performance in the form of high stakes assessment with total accountability placed on the child through the school and teacher. Capacity, defined as the ability of schools to change systemically and structurally to enhance instructional delivery used to operationalize OTL standards, was ignored. Testing became the accepted measure of reform's success and the means of establishing accountability, despite the inequities testing was to underscore and the costly OTL standards that had been created to ameliorate it.

School accountability was thus translated into obtaining higher test scores on state and national standards-based assessments, as standards-based tests are one of the most powerful policy levers that elected officials and policymakers have for influencing what happens in the classroom, and compared to other interventions they are inexpensive.

Nonetheless, standards-based reform continues unabated, despite the demise of the most important OTL standards, those favoring standards insisting that:

Standards improve student achievement and create high expectations by defining curriculum and its outcomes;

Standards are necessary to create equality of opportunity so that all students are on an even playing field;

Standards serve to synthesize school district efforts for improvement;

Standards and their assessments provide specific information to students, parents, and the community about achievement and progress.

Conservative reformer Diane Ravitch stated that it is impossible to lead anyone without a destination and in the absence of an agreement by educators; standards define the destination. Other proponents of standards claimed that standards have contributed to an overall positive tone on the national educational agenda, as never before has the national commitment to education been so vibrant, inclusive of all races and socio-economic classes of students. Both major political parties have championed a "world-class" education for students.

Those opposing standards assert that the standards movement is more useful for political posturing than it is to effect real change, claiming:

Standards assume that student achievement was not already high, so in some schools becoming better is thwarted by a focus on minimum performance;

Top-down mandates are a poor way to effect real change, representing heavy-handed regulation that has been a historically poor way to effect change. Notorious for unfunded mandates, state and federal education agencies enact regulation they cannot regulate or refuse to pay for. Thus, school reform is more effective when decision making is closest to the student;

Resources (capacity) are not equal and students do not have the same preparation for school, so one uniform set of standards is a recipe for failure at the outset. Regressive practices have been retrenched, reinforced by the assumption that higher expectations will naturally cause teachers and their charges to rise to meet them. Raising the bar of expectations, however, causes those with the least social and educational capital to be forced to leap higher, and then fall harder. There are other means of measuring student achievement besides a high stakes test.

Educators argue the methods used and organizational consequences of standards-based reform, but rarely take into account the unanticipated consequences that it has wrought. Education's national discourse has narrowed to a focus on testing, while obscuring the conversation on the purposes of education. There is a dearth of ideas to address this critical issue as exemplified by the negation of child development theories that speak of the importance of children's play and its importance in developing intentionality in favor of standards-based reform that has sometimes eliminated recess for the sake of academic "drill and kill" exercises.

Standards-based reform has led to an increase in grade retention. For example, in June of 2004, the mayor of New York City "left back" thousands of third graders who failed preliminary testing that was meant to determine how these students would do on the state-mandated testing program in grade 4, despite his being advised that research indicated retention is not at all successful, but, in fact, causes high school dropouts.

Failure of the grade 4 tests, however, means state meted punishment against schools and teachers. By screening who takes the high stakes state test, the potential for failure and its aftermath is thus abated. Other states have also taken this road to improve their scores. Many in education agree that the acclaimed "Texas Miracle" produced by Secretary of Education Rod Paige when he headed the Houston school system, where test scores jumped dramatically from one year to the next, indeed used this methodology. Placement into special education has increased, and tracking has taken on new importance, as loopholes that omit testing for students in the lower functioning stanines remain open. These examples are not what standards-based reformers had envisioned, but nonetheless have become practice to prepare the lowest achievers for high stakes tests (or eliminate them from participating), while at the same time pumping up scores to avoid sanctions. Laura McNeil, an anti-standards proponent, offered that with ethnic and racial diversity on the rise, the experiences of minority children have been discounted and marginalized and their language barriers further heightened. The predominant culture intensifies its demands further reducing the value of what minority children bring to the classroom. The use of high stakes tests as reform's "silver bullet" to improve schools has swept the nation while ignoring differences among children in favor of a "one-size-fits-all" solution. Safe schools, small class sizes, improved teacher compensation, long overdue systemic and structural reform, equity among schools, and curricula that engage children in the excitement and joy of learning took a backseat to testing. The enormous variations in school readiness and capacity, particularly among poor children and children of color, make this an improper moment to champion a homogenized system based only on assessments outcomes. The failure of the system at large is now easily located within the student, obviating any organizational shortcomings. This flawed logic fueled the notion that our educational system could be fixed with tougher standards that memorialize the practice of strict discipline and quantity over quality. Assessments are unlikely to enhance equity unless the mission of assessment is changed from a sorting function to one of diagnostic support. Their use as external monitors of schools, students, and teachers rather than locally generated tools for deep inquiry into teaching and learning leaves their long-term effect questionable. Thus, the standards-based reform process makes education the "great stratifier" as opposed to the "great equalizer."

What about the affective fallout of standards-based and high stakes assessed reform?

Susan Ohanian suggested a link between the increase in Attention Deficit Disorder (ADD) diagnoses and the standards movement. Since 1990 the number of children diagnosed with ADD increased from 900,000 to 5 million, with a 700 percent increase in Ritalin production. Ritalin, a drug in the amphetamine family, is prescribed for ADD to control attention span and hyperactivity in children.

Regulating the passive learning of children objectifying them as hostages rather than learners suggests a lack of basic respect. A new pedagogy (models, strategies, and methods) that respects children's unlimited potential must replace current views of children's success as measured by time oriented and tested curriculum. Alfie Kohn suggests that an obsession for numbers has produced poorly constructed tests that assume a single correct answer to problems. They measure how good kids are at recognizing information, not generating it, emphasizing isolated learning, not the integration of facts and ideas. The constructivist value of learning by coming across an essence of something unexpected, something that cannot be easily explained, or something that stimulates a change in a belief is to accommodate true learning. Extrinsic regulation intrinsically limits motivation.

Standards reinforce the bureaucratic control model by championing specialized and differentiated work roles and a top-down hierarchy of decision making. Instruction breaks down knowledge into a curriculum composed of discrete subjects. Linda Darling-Hammond argued that the problem is that standards empower dysfunctional organizational structure that invests inadequately in the knowledge and tools required to address student needs. Schools remain structurally and systemically the same as they were since the 20th century began, incorporating standards-based reform as they would have any other incursion.

It is my thinking that the practice of democracy in giving students a voice in the direction and meaning their learning will take is a powerful argument that challenges the rigidity fostered by standards-based reform, though I admit freely this is not a new idea. The Progressive Education Association initiated the famous Eight-Year Study in 1932. Staffs from fifteen public and private high schools concluded that their central purpose was to give students "an understanding and appreciation for the way of life we call democracy." In essence, learning became student-centered in these schools, rather than centered solely on college admission. After college graduation, an assessment of the success of the students of the fifteen experimental schools was compared to a control group. It was found that the graduates of the experimental schools did better in college than the comparison group. Further, those students from the most radically changed of the experimental schools did appreciably better. The louder students talked, the better they did in the short-term, and, more importantly, in the long-term. Democracy and self-motivated ambition proved itself feasible in the educational arena, contradictory to heavy-handed mandates that claim to improve student outcomes. This case strongly suggests that standards-based reform can do little to sustain the student's ontological long-haul, serving only the political short-haul.

The personalizing of education is important to kids who want to maintain their dignity and worth, something standards-based reform tends to negate. Students want teachers to recognize who they are, to listen to what they have to say, and to respect their efforts. In classrooms where personalities are allowed to show, students respond more fully, both academically and personally. Initial differences in attitudes students have about themselves and their place in school that challenge family or SES expectations about their futures are exacerbated by the practice of tracking. Tracking as previously mentioned is an unanticipated outcome of preparation for high stakes assessment that characterizes standards-based reform. To "lower track" students, this practice leads to a cycle of failure. As students age, anxiety about promotion and high school graduation is heightened by continually poor test scores, producing depressed feelings of self-worth. All of this occurs a time when U.S. students are the most tested in the world, taking more than 100 million standardized tests each year.

Surveys I've reviewed that were administered to students over thirty years ago are almost carbon copies of those administered two or three years ago as their view of education as being limited in a participatory sense and of questionable efficacy is not an emerging phenomena as reported by the study conducted in 1973. Researchers surveyed 10,000 high school seniors in twelve ethnically diverse northwest Indiana high schools ranging in size from 500 to over 1675 to determine the degree of student alienation. Over half of the students saw little relationship between what they learn in school and outside life or found the school experience contradictory to out-of-school learning, twenty-five percent saw regulations as overbearing, twenty percent had no pride in their experiences and did not talk with their parents about school work, and eighteen percent found no aid in solving personal problems. Two in five students saw teachers doing the planning and telling students what to do. The outcomes of standards-based reform indicate that non-contextualization, irregularities, and inequities students saw almost thirty years ago exist and are intensified today.

A 1998 study used a narrative form to discuss issues of school reform with the researchers' own children. What drove their research was an attempt to understand the resistance and lack of progress toward meaningful educational change within a postmodern framework, rather than responding to the usual technical-rational philosophy and mandates imposed by state and federal bureaucracies. The authors noted the absence of student voice and its connection to the obvious lack of engagement and subsequent indifference or blatant resistance toward the comprehensive high school curriculum. They found that while teachers are fiercely dedicated to their young charges, many continue to teach with outdated instructional strategies based on lecture or "banking" methods (as defined by Paolo Freire in his book Pedagogy of the Oppressed, where teachers expound the standards-based truth as the state has deemed it to be, and students accept it as such, not even to question its authenticity or value in the present tense). Students praised teachers who listened to and respected what students thought, and challenged them to think. The authors concluded that perhaps the adults were really not in charge, that students manage to exercise resistance to all efforts to manage and direct their lives, just as Philip Cusick had determined in his 1973 book *Inside High School.* Not surprisingly, teachers reported feelings of isolation and frustration similar to that of students. The student informants who took part in providing me the data for my dissertation spoke along similar lines, valuing extracurricular accomplishments and courses with small classes that provided an intimacy with their teachers over those courses that were preparation for New York State testing. They also expressed the feeling that their teachers were at once their champions, yet victimized as they were by standards-based curriculum and high stakes testing that narrowed the scope and sequence of their pedagogy.

One may ask at this juncture, "So, where's the reform?" Ginette Delanshere of Indiana University offered in the Teachers College Record in 2002 that state assessments are poorly constructed, not bearing a hint of how students know. They do not break the 100-year-old mold of assumptions about teaching and learning that have underscored educational practice. Yet, we persist. At least the tests showed in plain numbers that we have problems, many of which were already known or at least suspected. If we make a grand assumption that state exams have a degree of validity and reliability, they are confirmed.

Now, for the Double Jeopardy question: What do we do about it, besides testing again and again, and with each test, coming up with the same results? If a particular state's test results show improvement for a particular grade of children, why aren't the results comparable at the next testable grade level? Why haven't test scores on other measures increased, such as the SAT, ACT, and NAEP, if state test scores show improvement? Half the answer is that we are teaching kids to take tests along the narrow slice of information state tests are designed to highlight, not teaching them to think. The other half is a bit more complicated, as we shall see.

Chapter 4
"And we're living here in Allentown..."

More on one of my favorite composer's piece later, but let it be said at this point that Billy Joel's *Allentown* speaks volumes of the systemic failure of education. Joel's own experiences mirror the inflexibility of a system that becomes more brittle with time and legislation. He said in a TV interview I saw a few years back that the professional staff in his high school somewhat shunned him because they favored kids who desired to go to Columbia University while it was his intention to go to Columbia Records. Billy didn't fit the system's mold, it seems, just like an increasing number of kids do not because of the overwhelming reliance on testing of a narrowed assessment-driven curricula by which the system judges a student's total worth and abilities.

There is bad news and good news about No Child Left Behind (NCLB). First the good news: Through mandated testing, NCLB made us acutely aware of the horrific inequities and failed promises that are routinely accepted as the cost of doing business for poor kids and minority kids. Now the bad news—the only thing we are able to offer them is more tests. Now the worse news—the program is under funded, and the funds that are being used aren't making kids any smarter, abler, or empowered. But, boy, are those kids learning to pass tests! Then again, is this what we're all about?

I found the following article in *USA Today* on August 10, 2004. Although written about the goals of a college education, it speaks to our current K-12 situation.

"A Valuable Education"

I reject what I see as the implicit, "you-are-what-you-earn" premise of *USA Today*'s article, "The 'major' dilemma," and the opinions of Paul Harrington, one of the co-authors of *College Majors Handbook* (Life, Thursday). The book's authors suggest that majoring in such subjects as philosophy or literature has little value in our society because they don't help a person get a good job. This is the worst form of crass materialism. Unfortunately, it infects too many students, parents and employers.

I studied philosophy at Harvard College because I wanted to figure out what was true and moral. I went on to get a master's degree in philosophy. I now earn a substantial income as a management consultant, and I run my own business.

I'm often asked how my background prepared me for the work I do now. I learned to think. I studied values. I can discern patterns and form valid generalizations. I can communicate with senior management and workers alike. I learned to question, and I learned to listen.

Many advise, "Do what you love, and the money will follow." I couldn't agree more. We should stop trying to prepare kids for a career. I don't think society is well served...getting a good job.

James H. Davis
Cary, N.C.

Mr. Davis seems to unwittingly agree with Elliot Eisner of Stanford University, who stated in an article of the May 2003 Phi Delta Kappa that, to his mind, the major aim of schooling is to enable students to become the architects of their own education so they can invent themselves during the course of their lives. How might this be interpreted?

Mr. Davis' perception of the true meaning of the educational experience is one that champions the liberal arts. That he sees it as the best method to teach kids the parcels of skills that make up true learning as the best form of career development is applicable in this treatise as well, as an emphasis on discreet subject-specific standards does not open the mind to alternatives or interdisciplinary possibilities. The phrases of his epistle that I found most poignant speak voluminously to the ideas I'm framing in this work- I wanted to find out what was true and moral; I learned to think; I learned to question, and I learned to listen. These are incredibly hard concepts to measure, this to think, to question, to listen, because they are processes whose outcomes are not simply manifested as the right answers on standards-based high stakes tests; these skills transcend each and every discipline. In too many instances, not all mind you, we are narrowing our teaching so that kids pass a test by administering discreet bits of data to be memorized, without centering our teaching on kids becoming the solvers and initiators of questions. Principals seem to agree. In the March 17, 2004 edition of Education Week, Kathleen Kennedy Manzo reported on a poll taken of principals that indicated a narrowing of instructional methodology and topics to test-specific items, with the deepest erosion taking place in schools with high-minority populations. If any kids need to learn Mr. Davis' mantra, it is them.

Standards set minimums that are measured by tests. In setting minimums, we mandate everyone will meet that minimum, while we let the maximums, the special talents everyone has, to either be set at minimums, or ignored. In today's climate, if it is not tested, it is considered unimportant, as unimportant, say, as the liberal arts are to those who would want to insure we train kids for careers, not life. "Do what you love" is considered a no-no, a non sequitur to career formulation.

In schools, we hope kids ask questions and listen, even though it is the teacher who is asking most of the questions. We mistakenly assume the kids are thinking when they do ask questions. What gets lost is the fact that we grade them on what we want them to think, what we want them to listen to, and thus define the learning context by limiting the concepts of their questions. How do we then let them "do what they love" or find out what they love by limiting these ventures in the zeal to mandate and standardize what they do? Worse, when our testing indicates they weren't thinking, listening, or questioning appropriately according to the standards, we intensify the process by further limiting their own thinking, listening, and questioning opportunities in the things they want to pursue so they can eventually pass the test without further remediation, or by being denied high school graduation.

What gets lost in all of this is the fact that thinking, listening, and questioning are social functions; that is, you need to have someone else around whose interests are similar to yours so you can run your thoughts and questions by them to determine their validity and expandability. More so, you have to listen intently to the responses if you are really seeking answers. In standards-based classrooms, the person we rely on too much to do this is the teacher. The problem here is that the teacher is teaching what is mandated and doing it in the context of getting his or her kids prepared to answer the discreet questions on a high stakes exam that will determine if his or her school is to be sanctioned for failure to provide average yearly growth. There is very little pedagogical "wiggle room," especially if the teacher happens to be in a school where English is the second language for a lot of the kids, or the kids are so poor that they have very little social or cultural capital to expend that is congruent to what the standards and assessments demand. The short of it is that poor kids don't have the same access to knowledge as rich kids, as their ability to experience different essences of knowledge is limited by the lack of their economic capital.

For example, there are kids who look at a picture in a book of the Mona Lisa and are asked to describe it. Then there are kids who actually saw the Mona Lisa up close and personal, and not only can describe the painting, but the entire context of the Louvre and the other paintings they experienced that appear in their texts, as well as the whole experience of visiting and engaging an entirely different culture authentically. It's akin to someone telling you a joke that flops, and the jokester then responds, "Ah, it was funnier the first time. I guess you had to be there."

Kids who don't speak English have cultural issues they need to deal with, plus the fact that their language reflects another completely different culture with different meaning for different phrases, behaviors, and happenings. That, in turn, makes their learning curve a bit longer. They are not less capable. Poor kids have the same brainpower as rich kids. So do kids who don't speak English. Their learning difficulties are grounded in their limited awareness of the world as the majority knows it, and it is the majority who holds the academic power to test knowledge of the world as it defines it to be. Poor kids and non-English speakers are limited by their experiences as to what they can understand as readily as other kids. Their physical and social needs may inhibit the speed of their learning as well.

I can hear it already: there are those reading this that are thinking or saying, "My parents and grandparents were poor, and I learned!" I also hear, "My grandparents came here speaking no English. They did okay!"

Well, hooray for you and me.

My parents and grandparents were Italian immigrants. They too were poor. However, they were literate in their own Italian language, and that made English easier to acquire. They were also skilled tradesman, which made earning a living a bit easier. While my parents and grandparents lived in an Italian ghetto, my parents moved out of it in the 1950s and into the multi-ethnic suburbs that Mr. Levitt created. Many of the kids who come to us as immigrants today have virtually no education and their parents have no formal training in any trade or craft, as the roots of international poverty are deeper than many of us realize. In one high school in which I worked, there were recently immigrated students who were seventeen years old and had never gone to school in their native El Salvador or Nicaragua (the reader with an astute historical sense will remember we were involved in some conflicts there about fifteen years ago that left both countries in social and economic shambles—another one of those coincidences). And now, as always, it isn't the land owners or businessmen who come to America—it is the poor (it's all on the base of that Statue in New York Harbor—you know, the poor, the tired, the huddled masses yearning to be free. Ellis Island wasn't a pleasure cruise stopover for rich Europeans on a U.S. tour. The rich Mexicans and Central Americans are staying in Mexico and Central America as well.)

If you are not convinced immigrant children are not learners, assuming that poor English skills are akin to stupidity, a report National Foundation for American Policy published is a report by Stuart Anderson on their website (HYPERLINK http://www.nafp.net)www.nafp.net) entitled The Multiplier Effect, in which the author claims that sixty-five percent of the top science students and sixty percent of all the top math students are children of immigrants. In addition:

Seven of the top ten award winners at the 2004 Intel Science Talent Search were immigrants or their children. (In 2003, three of the top four awardees were foreign born. In fact, in the 2004 Intel Science Talent Search, more children (eighteen) have parents who entered the country on H-1B (professional) visas than parents born in the United States (sixteen). To place this finding in perspective, note that new H-1B visa holders each year represent less than 0.04 percent of the U.S. population, illustrating the substantial gain in human capital that the United States receives from the entry of these individuals and their offspring (p. 16)

Another astounding note: If those who opposed immigration had succeeded over the past two decades, two-thirds of the most outstanding future scientists and mathematicians in the United States would not be in the country (p. 17).

As with most issues, there are two sides. Some immigrant children may need more help than others, but the rewards of taking care of kids far exceed policies of exclusion. It is also proper to note here that today's poorest ghettos are Hispanic and African American, but the white kids who are growing up in Appalachia are at no better advantage—poverty and socialized crime against children are non-racial and non-ethnic; so much for equity. However, as muted as equity's voice seems to be, let it be known that The College Board's annual SAT report indicated that thirty-seven percent of the record 1,419,007 SAT-takers in the Class of 2004 were minorities, the highest percentage ever. The kids want to succeed. Imagine if we empowered them and their thinking just a bit more.

Blaming kids for their lot is just unfair. How many parents when disciplining their children hear the remark, "I didn't ask to be born!" Well, neither did poor kids, Hispanic kids, or African American kids. They don't revel in the pain of their plight to make us angry and illogical. A kid with a bad "yesterday" and "today" doesn't hold out much hope for "tomorrow." Be that as it may, there is no reason we should not expect that any kid couldn't excel in some context, or in several. In fact, we should demand it, and we should be most intolerant in accepting anything less than their best efforts. However, the process and setting of education need a major injection of eduprise, what I define as a bold, sustaining foray into the "how" and "what" of education; the need to reflect an aggressive, new-found sense of urgency and support for all kids. Clearly, we know there are the learning gaps that high stakes tests, their reliability and validity notwithstanding, have demonstrated. Systemically, we have no clue how to close them, in a large part because we are thinking within the framework of the current structures and systems of the age-old educational process.

Paolo Freire, a Brazilian whose work with teaching Brazilian peasants literacy, offered a critical pedagogy for education. By "critical," it is meant to infer that those being educated have something to say about themselves that tells of their worth in the process of learning. They are beings in the world, although the world of power does not recognize them. To Freire, schools were political sites that either engaged people in informed political participation to empower democracy and the future, or prevented them from becoming engaged. That schools have increasingly become political sites can only be reinforced by the origination of the standards-based high stakes test reform effort that arose from A Nation At Risk. Freire's belief in literacy as a means to democracy was summed up best by his simple concept that to read the word was to read the world.

"What is your word?" This is the question that served as Freire's inquiry resulting in the birth of literacy as a form of agency for Brazilian peasants. He cast aside prepared materials that meant nothing to them, and instead employed their contextual vocabulary that explored their being and its intentionality. Hearing their words was hearing their world. Perceptions (one person's meaning) become conceptions (socially constructed meanings through dialogue).

Freire's concepts bear discussion as they pertain to the context of this writing. In his book Pedagogy of the Oppressed, a standards-based "package" represents knowledge and is actualized as a gift bestowed by those who consider themselves knowledgeable upon those they consider to know nothing. The more students work at storing the deposits entrusted to them, the less they develop the critical consciousness which would result from their intervention in the world as transformers of that world. As he stated:

The more completely they accept the passive role imposed on them, the more they tend to the world as it is and to the fragmented views of reality deposited on them. They are not beings for themselves. Students are not engaged in dialogue, as no oppressive order would permit the oppressed to begin to question, very simply: Why? (p. 86).

Freire judged that political and educational reforms have failed because their authors designed them according to their own personal views of reality as society's power elites, never once taking into account (except as the objects of their actions) the beings-in-the-world to whom their program was ostensibly directed. To Freire, dialogue is the theory characterizing an epistemological, socially constructed relationship that establishes a way of learning and knowing through the practice of conversation. He saw the role of educator as a directive authority with an active presence, but not an authoritarian who would deny the active role of the learner, as standards-based reform essentially does. This experience of sharing of ideas through dialogue establishes a social construction of knowledge. As Freire put it, "It implies curiosity in the process of coming to voice."

Freire's concept of conscientization makes us aware of our kids' "unfinishedness." It makes for education possibilities based on "I wonder" rather than simply "I do," allowing for fresh combinations of information and ideas. From Freire's perspective, standards-based reform has relegated the concept of student intentionality to a secondary role. Combined with the practice Freire identified as assistencialism, which is to view those who question empowered authority as requiring assistance, the denial of intentionality becomes complete. One New York State superintendent, for example, could not control a parent rebellion of sorts in his district when they kept their children home on state testing day. It was their statement that the testing program had no merit for their children. The state's commissioner of education asked the superintendent for data and explanations that amounted to a punishment assignment.

It is the controlling view of the standards-based reformer that attacking symptoms serves the purpose, disregarding the causes of social ills as the real problem. It is a concept much akin to the Native American term of shape shifting; that is, to show a change in appearance or character for the purposes of deception. This harkens back to the rebuttal of the vastly broader OTL standards that were disregarded by educational reformers who accepted narrowed curriculum and high stakes tests only as the instruments that would transform America's schools. The student has become the complete passive object, a victim if you will, incapacitated to decide the path to follow and denied the conditions that develop intentionality, all in favor of political control based on the premise of educational reform through mandated quantification.

Freire used the concept of massification as the reliance on educational models and methods that denies the development of individual agency. To do this, it relies on specific, directed curricula that demand the neutralization of critical consciousness. Massification separates curriculum into bits where the student has his or her activity limited, yet exaggerated by subject-specific specialization, much like high schools have done since the early 1900s. Students see limited application of their standards-based learning to "the real world," and recognize little relevance from subject to subject within the structure of the standards-based high school. While standards-based reform did not create this contrivance, it certainly embraced it. Further, the art of dialogue becomes a dead-ended process, as the models and methods resulting from the implementation of standards-based reform embraces "the bells:" the bell that rings to dismiss kids from one arena of fragmentation, and the one that sounds to commence another.

Billy Joel's *Allentown* tells of ignoring the concept of voice and dialogue as a conduit to think, to listen, and to learn. The song tells of present day young men and women lamenting the good life the previous generation lived after World War II, when steel production was a major industry in Pennsylvania. Jobs were as plentiful as cheap oil, and the pay reasonably good. Pennsylvania coal fed the Pittsburgh blast furnaces. Sheet steel and rolled steel went to Detroit to build the new cars Americans bought every three or four years. Oh, those Volkswagens were cute, but no real threat.

Then somebody bought a Toyota.

The paradigm shifted, and the world was never quite the same again. Kids whose Allentown-esque high schools taught them the minimums they would need to work the furnaces, the mines, the auto plants, and the railroads faced unemployment because their jobs were gone and they didn't know how to do anything else. Worse, they didn't think they could do anything else. They never learned how to learn. The standards of the day did not prepare them for the next day, as they were geared to what the powers deemed important at the time and ever after; kind of like what's happening today despite the claims of "world class education." They did what they were told, as today's kids do, but as the song says, Our graduations hang on the wall, and they never really helped us at all. The idea of life-long learning in a critical sense—to think, to listen, and to question—was thought to be irrelevant. There would always be "iron, coke, and chromium steel." They knew nothing else as their education was marginalized by the powers that created the standards of the day as the standards for always, localized to ridiculous, narrow minimums. What they did know, nobody cared enough to ask about because a whole way of life became irrelevant practically overnight as those Toyotas multiplied and an era ended.

What the kids in Allentown received was the blame for doing what the powers asked. What was dumped on the rest of us was the nonsense in A Nation At Risk, which pinpointed that blame in a cowardly, manipulative surface-skimming manifesto that avoided taking responsibility by pedantically denying the depth of the truth. At most, that report demonstrated a tremendous command of the obvious, a pontificating diatribe of obvious failures. It was not a pathology of the errors made or a litany of solutions to make things better. At the least, it should have been an apology to kids for decades of failed foreign policy and pompously marginalized domestic policy that put them in the land of the lost called Allentown. You don't have to live in Brazil to be oppressed.

And still, at least educationally, "We're living here in Allentown."

Chapter 5
FDR, A Five-Star, and The Army—
Their Effects On School Reform

The federal government's intervention in education has a long history. The Morrell Act created land grant colleges (such as the Pennsylvania State University) to provide education for the frontier, and West Point and Annapolis (The United States Military Academy and the United State Naval Academy) were created to provide our then fledgling country with engineers who could construct the west and protect its inhabitants, and a creditable naval supremacy that valued educated officers to stave off European threats. While these institutions were in themselves a statement of federal purpose, in my estimation, the GI Bill of Rights was probably the single most important piece of legislation that transformed the United States into the economic and military power that became the envy of the world.

The GI Bill has an interesting history. It was proposed by President Franklin Delano Roosevelt in one of his famous "fireside chats" on July 28, 1943 in the midst of World War II, on the heels of the collapse of Italian fascism marked by the resignation of the dictator Benito Mussolini. FDR's speech that evening provided a listing of benefits the veterans of World War II should come to expect after the cessation of hostilities. Initially, Roosevelt wanted to insure that the returning vets would not find themselves in breadlines or victims of chronic unemployment, a repetition of the Great Depression from which he had struggled to lift the nation at the beginning of his multiple terms as president. He said, "I have assured our men in the armed forces that the American people would not let them down when the war is won." FDR mentioned six promises he intended to keep to his heroes, the first two involving unemployment insurance until a job was found, and mustering out pay to cover the period between discharge and employment. Two of the last three suggested a new role for government—old-age survivor benefits, improved provisions for hospitalization, and sufficient pensions for disabled soldiers, sailors, and marines. The third and last promise, however, was the most profound. "...An opportunity for members of the armed services to get further education or trade training at the cost of the government."

The Serviceman's Readjustment Act of 1944 was signed into law on June 22, 1944 sixteen days after D-Day in France and eleven days after D-Day in the Pacific's Mariana Islands, two of the bloodiest days in our military history. The bill would provide tuition, fees, books, subsistence, and educational materials for veterans, and the freedom to attend an educational institution of the veteran's choice. Colleges were encouraged to admit the veterans who met their admission requirements despite the statement made by the then president of the University of Chicago, who claimed it would turn the colleges and universities of the country into "hobo jungles." Within seven years, 8 million veterans received educational benefits. Of that number, 2.3 million attended colleges and universities, 3.5 million received school training, and 3.4 million received on-the-job training. By 1951, the cost to the federal government was $14 billion dollars.

The GI Bill produced engineers and technicians needed for the budding technological economy, and teachers for the "baby boom." For the colleges, crowding campuses precipitated a building binge of classrooms and new dormitory facilities. Curricula expanded. Teaching staffs enlarged and summer courses thrived. The age of the students on campus broadened from the traditional eighteen to twenty-three year-olds, and a new seriousness of purpose was implanted by those who so recently lived with war's horrors and desperately wanted a better life for themselves and in the memory of their absent buddies. The social practice that considered higher education to exist only for the privileged few was shattered. The mainstream population of America's colleges was broadened forever, transforming society by opening the door to higher education to those who had previously been disenfranchised. The economic effects are immeasurable. As any veteran will tell you, the GI Bill was the greatest piece of legislation ever enacted. It created the world's greatest economic and industrial engine.

However, new threats abounded. In 1957, the Soviet Union launched Sputnik, the world's first artificial satellite (a few years earlier, they successfully tested a hydrogen bomb). As its orbital path took it across the United States, Americans grew queasy at the thought that an enemy had formally violated their airspace and could unleash untold horror on them from space and they could do nothing about it. What was worse, each attempt to launch an American satellite ended in a catastrophe marked by the sight of a rocket blowing up after rising a few feet from the launching pad. President Dwight D. Eisenhower was under tremendous pressure to respond. The "Red Scare" mentality of the 1950's was at a fever pitch with Russia's apparent technological supremacy. It would have been politically astute for the former five-star general and liberator of Europe to clench his teeth and demand more planes, missiles, bombs, and tanks to challenge the Soviet menace. Instead, Eisenhower went to his roots at West Point, where he was trained to be an engineer as well as an army officer. He problem-solved for the long-term, and decided what would catch and then dominate and surpass the Russians would be an emphasis on math and science education to produce engineers, scientists and technicians, better trained teachers and counselors, and facilitated college access for those who would perform these tasks. With what became the National Defense Education Act (NDEA), Eisenhower not only set the stage for dominance in space, but also laid the foundation for winning the Cold War (I am told by friends in aerospace that the advent of the B-2 Stealth Bomber was the final straw to the Soviet Union's collapse, as to create a defense against its virtual invisibility would cost the Soviets trillions they didn't have.)

While the NDEA was a huge success, using the powerful lens of historic hindsight, a wrong structural and systemic turn was made here. James Conant, a Harvard professor and famous chemist, headed a study to reform high school practice. In order to make the best use of the country's math and science resources, Conant suggested that the small high schools that dotted the country should be eliminated in favor of large, comprehensive high schools. Students who wanted to pursue studies in math in science could be exposed to the best educational facilities, practices, and teachers. Hard-to-find math and science teachers (these are areas where it is still difficult to recruit teachers) could be concentrated rather than spread out. Students pursuing vocational studies would also be exposed to the best available equipment. The economy of size that the large high schools would produce would make them more effective.

Consider that Conant was a cold warrior who was witness and participant to the incredible manufacturing feats that became commonplace in winning World War II, and the pressure of the Cold War no doubt was somewhat abated by returning to themes and practices which had proven track records. During World War II, shipyards were turning out liberty ships at the rate of one per day. Thousands of aircraft were built in factories that previously built automobiles, or in brand new factories that were erected overnight. The Manhattan Project turned nuclear theory to practice, producing the atomic bomb in three years and creating new technologies and heretofore unheard of manufacturing techniques to create plutonium and isotopes of uranium. Efficiency through standardization with production techniques made for effective manufacturing outcomes.

This idea was errantly adapted to educating children in the most efficient setting as possible. Standardization of practice assumes kids do not vary, and while machines can be made uniformly the same, kids cannot and are not. Unfortunately, the large comprehensive high school proved to be not at all an effective structure, and a good deal of educational research and literature is presently dedicated to the systemic effectiveness of small schools over their large, impersonal counterparts. Conant should have been tipped off he was on the wrong track with this thinking when a survey he mailed to students to relate their experiences in large schools had a high non-response rate. Sometimes silent voices say the most. Nonetheless, Conant should be credited with initiating structural change. What didn't happen was any sample research or case studies on what might be wrought by making schools larger and less personal. There is no more personal business than education. Only surgery comes as close.

By the 1970s, our comprehensive high schools had become huge, impersonal warehouses, especially in the inner cities. Class sizes mushroomed and dropout rates soared, indicating that the theory of economy of size collapsed under the sheer weight of expanding populations, and comprehensiveness was an out-of-date term to describe an out-of-date system. Curriculum became departmentalized and disconnected. Students saw high school as regressive, non-caring, and even hostile. For much of the population, high school was a place to socialize. The high school was ripe for restrictive standards-based reform efforts that were politically aimed at centralizing curricula, instructional methods, and outcomes as a means of bringing a perception of order to a system totally out of control, with no specific mission, but a multitude of purposes. If curriculum could be standardized and quantification of the results could be instituted, the old structures might prove to be valid. This was thought to be the key to better schools.

How does standards-based reform compare to reform that literally changes schools, inside-out, top-to-bottom, as the best means to redefine the nature of the high school, reorienting its purpose, refocusing its intent, and heightening its accountability? The literature suggests that innovation is stifled while stale practice is reinforced.

Standards reinforce the bureaucratic control model by championing specialized and differentiated work roles, a top-down hierarchy of decision-making, and a formalization of goals and expectations into affectively neutral rules and codes of behavior. Instruction breaks down knowledge into a curriculum composed of discrete and fixed subjects, teaching with the aim of imparting specialized knowledge and instruction as organized into a standards-based and sequenced pattern within subjects. The organization of instruction into departments and tracks is consistent with a specialization model. As standards are subject-specific, this paradigm seems to strengthen. Linda Darling-Hammond of Stanford University argued that the problem is that standards empower dysfunctional organizational structure that invests inadequately in the knowledge and tools required to address student needs. The lot of the poor students and students of color worsened. Students of means were denied reform that would enhance their growth. Rather than pushing upwards, the "great middle" became greater, as the bar was not raised for most of the population. Because the structure of the school day and year did not change, and because schools remained structurally intact, the paradigm in use became ever more dominant.

For example, any innovative program that suggested a venture "outside the box" of the current model at the two large school districts in which I practiced was usually met with, "A great idea… but what about the buses?" Should buses be the dominant factor in determining educational excellence? Sadly, they are. Expensive, wasteful, but they are absolutely required because kids who live farther from their large comprehensive high school need to be transported to it. The bigger the schools and school district, the more dependent we become on the buses, and thus the more restrictive our programs become. Yet, parents cannot use them to visit their schools, nor can senior citizens, nor can anyone else. Through a variety of legalities and regulations, districts pay through the nose to run their own private bus lines that determine who can get to the school, when, and under what circumstances. And if they have to run on weekends, the costs become even more prohibitive. Summers are almost always out of the question. Early and late day runs are problematic as well.

While I am discussing government intervention in schools, the Department of Defense schools, those run for the dependents of military personnel on military bases, are interesting examples of what schools could be. The inclusion of community support and high expectations of a teaching staff integrated in decision making can overcome SES deficits that are laminated by high stakes tests. A study conducted in 2001 by researchers at Vanderbilt University accounted for the unusually high NAEP (National Assessment of Educational Progress) scores, especially for minority children, reported by middle schools run by the Department of Defense for the children of military personnel stationed in the United States and abroad. Minority students make up forty percent of the school's population, eighty percent come from enlisted personnel. Half of their student populations would qualify for free and reduced lunch programs in civilian public schools. Thirty-five percent transfer every year. Success lies in several factors. The post commanders offer the schools great support, inclusive of a standing "place of duty" order that specifies that parents will (not should) attend parent-teacher conferences. The sense of community fostered by a military post supports the schools and students well. Teachers have very high expectations of students, and enjoy a mix of top-down bottom-up decision making, and rigorous staff development. There is no need to use buses, as the schools are self-contained within the base's structure. Class sizes are small.

The military is seemingly all about education in very authentic circumstances. A speaker from the Army's recruiting unit came to speak at a graduate course I taught this summer of 2004. The young woman, a first lieutenant, had completed college on an Army ROTC scholarship. She had recently returned from duty in Kuwait and Iraq. She astonished me with her comment that ninety-three percent of all soldiers with the rank of Sergeant First Class, the middle level NCO rank, had completed Bachelor's degrees. Further, soldiers in Iraq and Kuwait were transported to Kuwait to take a course that would prepare them for the SAT. Education is constantly discussed within the Armed Forces, and there are many incentive programs to educate soldiers through a variety of venues and retain them within the ranks after their enlistments are up. The Army will not take a high school dropout as a recruit. While the services do not meet their recruitment goals, they turn away many who cannot score well on the Armed Services Vocational Aptitude Battery (ASVAB), a qualifying test that reviews aptitude and job skills that many educators consider a fine instrument.

It makes you think about the quick victories scored in liberating Kuwait, and how quickly formal resistance in Iraq was subdued (though guerrilla action may go on for years). Perhaps the Iraqi soldiers were not all that bad; perhaps it was because our soldiers were that good.

Without realizing it, the lieutenant also drove her discussion to the heart with the use of the words "my soldiers," as opposed to the more popular term "troops" when referring to army personnel. Troops seems an impersonal and general term. Soldier seems to give the individual more value as a person. Throughout her discussion, the lieutenant displayed absolute and personal ownership of those men and women under her purview on and off the battlefield. Leadership goes far beyond the ability to give orders and maintain discipline, far beyond the fancier uniform. It's as affective a practice in the army as it is in civilian affairs. This same concept is educationally relevant, especially among those who aspire to become administrators (more on this later).

Look at what great things government can accomplish when it stimulates, urges, encourages and awards, and funds edu-prise. When it manages schools without encouraging a change in structures or systems as Conant's report had done, and now how No Child Left Behind does, innovation is stifled. In her award-winning book *The Right to Learn*, Dr. Darling-Hammond writes:

Bureaucratic solutions to problems of practice will always fail because effective teaching is not routine, students are not passive, and questions of practice are not simple, predictable, or standardized. Consequently, instructional decisions cannot be formulated on high then packaged and handed down to teachers (p.103).

There is no doubt that schools needed to change. However, those most familiar with schools were never asked their opinions, and those individuals are teachers and kids. Those not associated with schools on a continuous basis cannot make judgments on the scope and sequence of reform. The landmark A Nation At Risk was formulated by a committee whose members included only one teacher, the one chosen by Ronald Reagan as teacher of the year. Conant never taught in the public schools. Legislation and money cannot abate all that is needed to be done. A complete structural and systemic overhaul is long overdue.

Chapter 6
What Do The Kids Say?

The concepts of school organization and structure need to be addressed to include the student's voice as the primary method of truly reforming schools. The voices of our clients, the students, should be heard with much more amplification than the current control setting provides. This chapter seeks to explain the power of the unheard student voice in a vocabulary that specifically speaks of their ontology.

Why listen to children? Children are products of our social, cultural, and historical acts. We as a society operationalize through our actions what a child is. How they arrive at their actions is an interpretation of our actions. They are mindful and constantly engage in self-conscious activity and provide us with their words to explain who and what they are. We must systematically seek out their discoveries and treat them seriously. How they see their world will give us deep insights on how our actions create their actions. In any serious reform effort, they deserve an active and meaningful role in determining the route their educational experiences will take. This is particularly antithetical to standardization, where children are objectified as inanimate and universally the same. Their knowledge may well contradict what adults claim to be "obvious."

Childhood may be described as that period of time in each person's life which society recognizes for the process of training, so as to become the kind of member that the society wants him/her to be. This is a new perspective, creating a conceptualization of how childhood is socialized.

In his book *Understanding Causality,* Jean Piaget defined the concept of "operations" as a set of transformations of the object world by the subject, giving children an intentionality and causality to their actions. Denying operations is to deny an opportunity for children to understand the interdependence and complexity of a large-scale society such as ours. By not asking children what they think and why, we are not only denying their agency, but in the long term, denying the validity of our own society. Kids are constantly negotiating their world with ours, trying to maintain a sense of themselves while adhering to the rules we thrust upon them. As any human would, they attempt to define themselves with power they can attain while keeping their sense of reality commensurate with the reality we interpret or create for them. But listening to kids describe their methods helps us to evaluate our methods in trying to provide them what we as adults feel is in their best interests.

Adolescents in particular have a tendency to resist any effort to disempower them, inclusive of passive instruction in pre-set materials, mechanical drills, and their exclusion in curriculum design. The constant efforts to produce standards-based outcomes clearly is an example of how adolescents might determine this action as being disempowerment, especially because it is centered on prepackaged knowledge that denies their dialogue, and that makes their own personal knowledge irrelevant. Indeed, sixty-five percent of high school dropouts who left school prior to the completion of eleventh grade saw no value in school, work, or had any ambition to the prospects of the future. Despite the mantra of standards-based reform, through its narrow, misdirected, and disempowering practices, too many see themselves as disenfranchised, and are indeed being left behind. What have students said in their words about their experiences through reform after reform? Though heard only in a whisper, there is a record.

Past school reform efforts have had political and economic implications, and have relegated democratic issues to secondary status. To this end, the literature suggests the muting of student voice is not new to education, and that students have historically viewed high school as non-engaging, non-contextual, repressive, and not at all preparatory for college or work. The control model that standards-based reform represents replicates what has not historically worked to change the structure or systems of high school in ways that engage the student in deep learning that engages the student's voice.

It would be incorrect to assume that processes of student marginalization originated in the present standards-based reform efforts. Researcher David Tyack and Larry Cuban at Stanford University have argued that students who were challenged with the "standards" of their day were forced to cope with structures and systems that were antithetical to them as students and human beings, very much in concert with today's standards-based and high stakes assessed reform effort. These researchers made a case to adapt schools to youngsters, rather than the other way around. They quoted an early twentieth century student:

School ain't no good. When you works a whole month at school the teacher gives you a card to take home that says how you ain't any good. And yer folks hollers on yer an' hits yer (p.108).

Another responded:

You never understands what they tells you in school, and you can learn right off to do things in a factory (p. 108).

At the turn of the last century students were described with terms such as dunce, shirker, loafer, reprobate, depraved, wayward, sluggish, and incorrigible. Through the 1950's, they were described as pupils of low I.Q., ne'er-do-wells, limited, laggards, backward, occupational student, and mental deviates. Today, they are described as handicapped, educationally deprived, culturally different, socially maladjusted, at-risk, and less fortunate. Throughout all time, the system and structures remained righteous and steadfast. The current standards movement intensifies what has not historically worked, still absolving structures and placing political power with the mainstream systems. Student voice is indeed muted, literally and figuratively.

It is pure denial to believe students do not think about what is happening to them as they travel through school. As Philip Cusik wrote in his book *Inside High School,* the premise that students assign any value to the things schools assert are important is a leap of faith, especially when their voice is not sought in making policy that affects them. The quality of school life for students is more likely to be determined by the social processes in schools than by objective quantities of things. To this, researcher Michael Fullan quipped about the outcomes that might arise if we treated the student as someone whose opinion mattered.

When kids are asked what they think, they respond in contrast to the mantra of standards-based reform. Sonia Nieto, in an article that appeared in 1994 in the *Harvard Educational Review,* noted that students became more disengaged as the curriculum, texts, and assignments became more standards-based, as there is often a tremendous mismatch between students' cultures and the culture of the school. Young people face innumerable personal, social, political, and economic challenges and structural changes not even dreamed about by previous generations. Schools need to focus on differences by setting appropriate instructional policies and practices if our collective will is to educate all students. In the words of a Vietnamese immigrant, Nieto quoted:

...If we go to school we want to a good job also, but we want to become a good person. Grades are not important to me. Important to me is education...I not so concerned about test scores very much...I just know I do my exam very good. But I don't need to know I got A or B. I have to learn more (p. 412).

Paolo Freire offered that in a more perfect world, those who speak regard those who listen as worthy to listen, and that those who listen regard those who speak as worthy to speak. Language is the place where actual and possible forms of social organization and their likely social and political consequences are defined and contested. It is where our sense of ourselves is constructed, but this construction is constricted in the teach-to-the-test pedagogy that has narrowed the classroom experience, and by eliminating discourse, retrenched the power in those who will listen. Language is a social production, and it is therefore not possible to think of language without ideology and without power. In other words, language is made effective by dialogue, and dialogue is a two-way street.

It is my thinking that the practice of democracy in giving students a voice in the direction and meaning their learning will take is a powerful argument that challenges the rigidity fostered by standards-based reform. There was a little-known but interesting study conducted in the years just prior to World War II, termed the Eight-Year Study. Initiated in 1932 by the Progressive Education Association, staffs from fifteen public and private high schools concluded that their central purpose was to give students "an understanding and appreciation for the way of life we call democracy." In essence, learning became student centered in these schools, rather than centered solely on college admission. After college graduation, an assessment of the success of the students of the fifteen experimental schools was compared to a control group. It was found that the graduates of the experimental schools did better in college than the comparison group. Further, those students from the most radically changed of the experimental schools did appreciably better. The louder students talked, the better they did in the short-term, and, more importantly, in the long-term. Democracy and self-motivated ambition proved itself feasible in the educational arena, contradictory to heavy-handed mandates that claim to improve student outcomes. This case strongly suggests that standards-based reform can do little to sustain the student's nature of being for the long haul, serving only the political short haul.

The research I conducted for my dissertation found that students treasured the opportunities when their teachers became mentors. I found that smaller learning environments fostered dialogue, and that the extracurriculum proved far more powerful a motivator than standards-based instruction. Though it was only one small study conducted by a fledgling researcher, it appeared that the kids found that their intentionality was fully operationalized in those structures that standards-based reform had not touched— and were the least expensive to operate. Kids involved with the US FIRST robotics program worked around the clock to complete their robot. They gave it form and "life" from a bunch of mechanical and electronic parts, within the competition's parameters. They and their teachers swapped knowledge, confidence, and incredible amounts of energy. Parents became involved and provided support in the form of pizza, cola, and cheers. The kids' and teachers' construction and operation of their robot proved the concepts of team learning could in fact be alive and well in a system that trumpets individual achievement over dialogue. Students had the same kind of feelings for the school dramatic arts clubs or the athletic teams they populated. It was here that they felt they were learning, in the company and mentorship of others. It's kind of like the way school ought to be.

An article that was published in the November 2000 *Teacher's College Record* by researchers Anne Whitlock, Damian Bebell, and Walt Haney painted a clear picture of the perceptions of kids and their experiences in taking the high stakes Massachusetts Comprehensive Assessment System (MCAS) exams. Younger children drew pictures, while older children wrote statements. The greater number of self-portraits created by the younger children depicted them as students who were anxious, angry, bored, pessimistic, or withdrawn from testing. The authors cite an American Educational Research Association (AERA) literature review that determined that contrary to the claims of high stakes testing acting to inspire student effort, it fails to motivate and worse, may trip negative results.

In New York State, the testing effort has taken on diabolical proportions. The passing rate on the high stakes Math A Regents exam at its first administration in June of 2003 was below twenty-one percent. The test is required for high school graduation. The state conducted a "review" that resulted in the state's negating the exam for seniors and juniors as a graduation requirement, but not for the sophomores. Instead, sophomores had their scores curved. Those who still failed were required to take the exam again. Special education students were allowed to take the older (and easier) Regents Competency Test (RCT) to meet the graduation requirement for math.

The same thing happened with the Regents Examination in Physics. Though not required for graduation, the state was forced to curve its results as well because of the very high failure rate. In fact, students who attained scores of three and four on the Advanced Placement exam, scores good enough to receive credit from the colleges to which they were accepted, had failed the physics exam.

What is the point of relating the above? Think for minute…what are the kids thinking about the efficacy of these exams? What are their teachers thinking, besides dealing with feelings of betrayal and malfeasance on the part of the New York State Education Department? And, what are parents thinking about the whole of it?

The fifty states of the union are pursuing their own versions of "world class standards." That means what is considered world class in New York is not considered world class in Florida, or North Carolina, or Massachusetts. New York will have incoming transfer students, including those who are unfortunate enough to transfer into a New York State high school as seniors, who will take the New York State Regents in Math A, English, and U.S. History. Even though their preparation is not in the New York State curriculum, they must pass the tests (and two others in World History and a science if they transfer in as ninth or tenth graders). They will not take the world-class standards of any other state as equivalent. What could be more unfair?

It is no wonder that the numbers of students opting to drop out of high school and pursue a high school equivalency diploma is growing. In 2002, forty-nine percent of those who earned a GED were teenagers, compared to thirty-three percent in 1992. Just as troubling is the fact that in 2003, there were 1.1 million kids being "home schooled," according the National Center on Educational Statistics, and the numbers are increasing. Of all students who entered ninth grade four years ago, only sixty-eight percent are expected to graduate. Schools have a confidence problem, and there is no standard that has addressed that.

Ginette Delandshere of Indiana University remarked in the *Teachers College Record* of November, 2002 that:

Although the call for change is clear, the proposals and recommendations being put forward have limitations of their own and are unlikely to yield the kinds of fundamental changes envisioned by researchers. These limitations lie either in the focus of the work, in the lack of a clear articulation of the theories and concepts, in the nature of the assumptions made about learning, many of which remain implicit or unchanged…that have remained deeply entrenched for more than a century (p.1461).

As Yogi Berra would say, "It's deja vu all over again." What might we expect from continuing the currently ineffective practices and formats? Probably more of those Toyotas, except now they are accompanied by more than a few of their high-end Lexus cousins.

Chapter 7
The Spider's Web of School Reform

Nothing is simple. That is, the simple things that need attention usually point to their own solutions and get themselves solved. To use simple solutions to address complicated problems, however, leads to heartache. That's because there are very few complicated issues that stand alone. Usually, the complicated issues involve the application of massive amounts of time and effort in an economic period of finite dollars that are intertwined with other complicated issues. This gives policy makers headaches. Political ramifications abound and usually define themselves in the context of liberalism or conservatism, both labels that are anachronistic vestiges of simpler times. As a result, we wind up with simple solutions that are, at best, compromises that treat the immediate problem, but let the causes fester. It's akin to treating symptoms, but not the disease itself.

In terms of educational policy, the problem is that we are running out of time and treasure in not doing the right thing, in a large part because we feel we need to stick to political labels—education is not a political problem. It would not be an understatement to say that it is a problem as fundamentally explosive to our national security as terrorism. That's the reason we wind up doing the cheaper interventional strategies because preventive strategies are too expensive—at first. Benjamin Franklin's adage about a stitch in time saving nine comes to mind. Ignoring problems or addressing them on the cheap without an overall plan for the long haul usually winds up with them rearing their ever uglier heads in the not-too-distant future. Compromise of late is not the best of both worlds, but the cheapest solution to address the pedantic concerns of those who call themselves liberals and conservatives.

Educational reform as an issue fits all of the above. The testing mania in which we are involved is not doing the job as advertised. Tests are becoming increasingly expensive, yet we avoid doing the real job of reform because policy makers believe they're getting a bigger bang for the limited, politically manipulated buck, but the bang they are hearing is the exploding cigar going off in their faces. We now have data (albeit with questionable validity and reliability), as it is collected from the results of a variety of tests with questionable reliability and validity that are given across the fifty states of the Union) that tell us that kids who are poor or culturally and ethnically distinct are having a hard time learning. We knew those kids had learning problems before we had the tests. We are now giving more tests hoping the scores go up by teaching to the test-specific items. Yet we are disappointed again and again by the results, as intensification doesn't work, nor will it ever work. What really needs to be done is restructuring and a redress of systemic paradigms in use, but this costs money. Do we raise taxes? Do we transfer funds from other programs that are also scrambling for dollars? Do we let failed ventures like charter schools and vouchers (read the research) continue because they are politically popular within the conservative ranks? Do we allow liberal diversity by individual school districts or states because we always have? Do we allow school privatization to continue when its results are dubious at best? Do we really think throwing more money at schools under the present circumstances will solve the problem? Do we adopt an attitude that basically says to kids, "If you learn it, all well and good. If you don't learn it...well, that's all well and good too." That was the attitude we had about a hundred years ago, and we rightly thought it too exclusive an idea in teaching our kids after World War II, when we had mandatory school attendance enacted throughout most of the land.

With this in mind, let's take a look at another thorny problem on the spider's web and its impact on school reform. I was astounded by a statement made by Bill Ford, the current CEO of Ford Motor Corporation a year or so ago: Ford spends more on health care than it does on steel. Think how profound that statement is! Ford Motor Company, a company that defined the industrial age in the United States, is crippled under the pressure of another social misfire that defies fixing. More of what you buy in your new Ford (and I would suspect your new Chevy or Chrysler) takes its value not from its basic components, but from a service twice removed from the consumer. As I edit this work, General Motors teeters on the brink of bankruptcy because of pension and health care outlays.

President Clinton had the vision to identify health care as a major siphon that draws off dollars in unproductive ways, as the health care system is inequitable and, as such, is interventional. The poor or unemployed without health care benefits only go to the doctor when their disease has progressed beyond simpler treatments. Children who aren't covered linger longer with illness, are susceptible to complications, and are increasingly absent from school. Sometimes the effects of their illnesses are longer term, or some illnesses need a longer treatment period. Losing a job means becoming deeper in debt if the worker becomes sick. Clinton's plan died because those opposing it were rigorously against government becoming bigger. I do not profess to be a constitutional scholar, but I remember something written by the Founding Fathers about "of, by, and for the people" when discussing the role of government. I would think that a solution to this problem comes under these auspices.

The news gets worse. *Newsday*'s August 22, 2004 edition indicated that since 2002 the ranks of poor Americans increased by 1.3 million, while the numbers of those lacking health insurance climbed even more, according to the U.S. Census Bureau. The number of people in poverty rose to 35.9 million. There are 12.3 million families with related children under the age of eighteen living in poverty, an increase of nearly six percent since 2002. These are the same children we claim shouldn't be left behind.

Let's start school reform here. What if we made it possible to cover all children from their pre-natal stages to age eighteen with health insurance? Further, what if we made it possible to have kids get annual checkups to determine their health on a regular basis, and made their medicines free? I would propose we extend this medical coverage to pregnant mothers, as prenatal care makes for a healthier baby whose capacity to learn would be substantially improved. What if we offered (better yet, mandated) pre-and post-natal parenting classes to these parents, so the negative behaviors in child rearing associated with poverty might be eliminated, and they could help their kids learn? What if the insured kids got at least two meals a day by keeping school cafeterias open on Saturdays and Sundays, and we made it possible for really needy families to have a subsidized meal per day? All of this would produce children more ready to learn, and make schools community centers of learning, rather than the foreboding "nine-to-three" institutions. To continue, preschool and daycare should be run on a sliding tuition scale in association with school districts to insure that kids are being prepared to enter kindergarten (which should be a full day program based on reading, socialization, and intentionality) ready to learn. Think about the incredibly high costs of special education, where mandated class sizes and restrictive labels are assigned according to the severity of a child's disability—might they be reduced because children were born and reared healthier, and the effects of poverty, while not eliminated, were reduced? Think in terms of dollars saved by reducing expensive mental and physical therapies and remedial programs that, at best, put educational patches on wounds born of social instability and inequity. Think in terms of kids who are not frustrated by school, but engaged by it in programs that can begin beyond the basics to address real learning difficulties. Successful kids lead successful adult lives, rather than lives of desperation that result from sustenance derived from the darker side of human activities. Think about how educating parents would make educating children more efficient and effective.

Here is something else to ponder: think about spending $60,000 for four years of tuition at a state university, rather than paying for one year of prison. A kid with a BA is not going to blow your brains out for the ten dollars in your wallet. Isn't it worth seeing a poor child at least get off to somewhat of an even start?

At a lecture given at the University of Virginia in April of 2004, William G. Bowen, President of the Andrew W. Mellon Foundation, discussed the medical crisis in the context of higher education. Citing a 2003 Brookings Institute study:

Over the past two decades, state funding of higher education has declined as a share of personal income. State appropriations have fallen from an average of roughly $8.50 per $1000 in personal income in 1977 to an average of about $7.00 per $1000 in personal income in 2002. Tuition increases have only partially offset the decline in state appropriations in allowing public institutions to keep up with private ones. As a result educational spending per full-time equivalent student has declined at public institutions from about 70 percent in 1977 to about 58 percent in 1996.

Why has this happened? In a word, Medicaid. Dr. Bowen continues:

Medicaid costs are projected to rise, and to rise dramatically; unless there is a sudden shift of the American people to pay for a larger share of the costs of health care among other things, at the national level, the prospects for reversing this funding trend are far from encouraging.

Keep this in mind, as Dr. Bowen continues:

...The major threat to continuing excellence of American higher education—even more important than present and potential funding constraints...I refer the state of public elementary and secondary education in America...Toward the end of the twentieth century...the rate of increase in schooling declined substantially in the United States. Improvement in the educational attainments of

cohorts of US natives born starting around 1950 slowed percepti-
bly. This slowdown has translated in a reduced rate of increase in
the educational level of the U.S. labor force starting in the 1980s.

It seems like the Allentown effect has some deep roots. In summary, Dr. Bowen concludes:

To continue to achieve excellence—defined, I repeat, as educating large numbers of people to a high standard and advancing and
disseminating knowledge—we must enrich the pool of candidates
for higher education by addressing equity objectives (pp. 204-
210).

I hope this aids the reader to see more clearly the circular nature and complicated web true educational reform represents. One
additional item: Alan Greenspan, the chair of the Federal Reserve,
raised the specter of the "baby boom" generation coming to knock
on Social Security's and Medicare's door in the next ten or so years.
In August of 2004, he raised the alarm that the nation might not
be able to meet its promised obligations to retirees. He warned
of "abrupt and painful choices" if Congress does not move to
trim benefits.

Does the nation want to keep the status quo on educating its
future workers, or does it want to take some powerful first steps
early on in a child's being to insure that no child – or any of us—is
left behind? Healthy, successful kids, educated to think, listen, and
question will be healthy, successful workers, and less dependent on
social programs and able to meet their obligations to those who
have done their share. Prevention is more effective and less expensive than intervention. And, it makes us all more successful. This is
the basis of edu-prise.

In terms of edu-prise, prevention in the form of producing
healthy learners makes a bold statement in seeing to the needs of
our kids while preserving society at large. It allows for dollars to
be well spent, and not re-spent inefficiently and ineffectively only
after crises appear. It also allows for schools to make interventions with families when children are still in their formative years,
and insure that early educational experiences are consistent
with learning.

General George Patton is quoted that he had anathema for paying for the same territory twice, that it was a waste of lives and
resources. That's why he would never retreat, even for possible
tactical advantage. Our present system of allowing "do-overs" and
patchwork to be central to our educational policy is as regressive
as Patton's view of retreating. If you haven't an altruistic bone in
your body for the plight of poor kids, or you think issues of equity
are better left to the philosophers to mull, certainly the idea of

spending more initially to spend less over time appeals to the most economy minded.

Educationally, the gap between rich and poor continues to grow. There are some heartening trends, as with the increase of SAT scores among Hispanic kids in 2004. Poor kids and parents don't know what to expect educationally, so they don't know what they don't know. Wealthy kids and parents know more. They have more economic, social, and cultural capital. Therefore what they don't know becomes refined and clearly evident, their issues and questions become more pointed and therefore more easily addressed as they are readily recognized. This is the nature of the educational gap. We treat the poor kids protectively, as we don't want anything worse to happen to them. The wealthy are treated more freely, as what happens to them becomes positive because they already know what they don't want to happen to them; this concept of stewardship for the young needs to be reexamined.

In the context of football, our system can be defined by comparing the roles of offense and defense. When you play defense, you prevent the other team from scoring, but mostly you don't score yourself. When you play offense, you score points. Perhaps a good educational reform offense would start by keeping kids healthy and ready to learn, as well as keeping their parents very much in the loop of our expectations.

When systems are preventively designed to ensure opportunity for enhancing equity, the rights of those who are better endowed are also enhanced because the system becomes prone to renewing and reinventing itself. As the bottom comes up, so do expectations. As a result, the top is driven higher to new, but unknown heights. Solving problems brings newer problems, but these problems are based on successes, not failures. They are problems that just don't happen due to neglect or interventional oversight, but are unintended outcomes of positive consequence. This, in turn, forces the organization to continually learn, thus providing new models to cope with new experiences. This is true reform in the mode of edu-prise.

Systems and structures based on intervention need constant resuscitation. Their dysfunction requires continuous attention, keeping them defensive and non-changing. We then design assessment systems that test quantifiable items of discreet, rote knowledge to make ourselves feel better about what the kids know, rather than create programs where kids can problem-solve and think critically, then tell us what they don't know. In essence, they are trained how to take a test, and little more. It becomes more expensive to resuscitate these regressive, interventional systems as time goes on, as individuals are kept as dependents rather than empowered to accede and succeed. If we don't produce healthier, brighter kids ready to learn literally at their start and hold their parents more accountable by supporting them in supporting their children, and if we choose to ignore the sources of their dysfunction by blaming them for their inabilities, and then altruistically patch them up with interventional nonsense rather than ensuring they are whole from the start, we remain defensive and interventional. We also stand on the brink of negatively changing the direction of our economy and our ability to compete internationally.

A social studies teacher once told me that Americans don't play defense very well. Even our armed forces play defense by playing offense. We score points, as our nature is to take risks and expand the envelope of what we know. That's how we got to be Americans in the first place, rather than staying British colonists. Yet, here we are in 2004, looking at the wrong end of the horse, because we think we're getting away on the cheap by attacking results, not causes, and thinking things will never change. This is the same reasoning that had someone choosing to buy the first Toyota over a Ford or Chevy forty or so years ago, and we've been scrambling to catch up ever since. It also explains how Billy Joel hit the nail on the head in explaining the pain of Allentown.

Chapter 8
Parents—Step Up To The Plate

Your kids need you. They need you now more than they ever did before. If you haven't noticed, the world has gone somewhat nuts. We cannot board a plane without submitting to a revocation of our rights, but we oblige because we know that there are miscreants who would take any opportunity to do us harm. We drive quickly over bridges and through tunnels. Teenage pregnancy remains a major problem. Two kids that nobody seemed to know one day became national villains the next when they shot up their high school and killed their fellow students in a Colorado suburb that was supposed to mirror the perfect place to raise a kid. Homicide is the leading cause of death for black males under the age of twenty-one. Are you scared yet?

Let me come right out and say it—you damn well know better, but you are letting your kids tell you what to do because many of you do not want to engage them. You skirmish with them, just like the rest of the educational system — yes, you are a part of it. Why? Because you're afraid your kid will take drugs if you are too strict, or they won't love you, or they'll go out and get pregnant or get somebody's daughter pregnant. You want to be considered a "cool" parent and you want your kids to like you. If this is you, you're being a sap, just like the rest of us in education.

Taking your kid to soccer and Little League games doesn't make you a competent parent. Engaging your child—YOUR CHILD—about his or her world, thoughts, and fears makes up for a good deal of what you cannot buy, acquire, or enlist. If you take a look at how some parents react at sporting events, you would wonder what goes on in the home if a child's game becomes a matter of

79

life or death. I've seen parents ignore pleas made by teachers and counselors to come in for academic conferences, but raise the devil when the child is suspended or given detention for an infraction of the school's disciplinary code. I've also seen parents completely obviate their roles, using the legislation of special education to put the entire blame on the school for their child's academic and social missteps. Remember, the kids spend at most eight hours with us, and sixteen hours at home – ostensibly with their parents. Then again, this mirrors society's modus operandi to intervene rather than prevent.

In one memorable parent-teacher conference I chaired, a teacher commented that the student could be doing so much better than barely passing her course if just a little more effort was forthcoming. The parent quipped, "He doesn't take drugs. He's home when he should be. That's all that matters. He's a good kid!"

My question, then as now, is…"Good for what?" Is not taking drugs the new denominator to measure success? Is it a "get out of jail free" card to produce slovenly academic work, yet expect it to be accepted? Will an employer one day consider him a successful employee because he doesn't take drugs, even though he does a lousy job? Will a fellow soldier admire him for his clean drug testing record as they share a foxhole under fire, or will he expect just a little bit more to insure they live another day? Will you forgive a poor brake job he performed on your car that caused you to rear-end another car at the first red light you came to after you left his repair shop because your brake repairman doesn't take drugs and comes home promptly after work?

Henry Louis Gates is the W.E.B. DuBois Professor of Humanities and W.E.B. DuBois Director of the Institute for African American Research at Harvard University. Dr. Gates is a humorously engaging and brilliantly articulate scholar who grew up poor in rural West Virginia, yet achieved enormous academic success. As a guest columnist in the August 1, 2004 *New York Times*, he wrote of Barack Obama's keynote address to the 2004 Democratic National Convention held in Boston where Mr. Obama remarked:

Go into any inner-city neighborhood and folks will tell you that government alone can't teach kids to learn. They know that parents have to parent, that children can't achieve unless we raise their expectations and eradicate the slander that says a black youth with a book is acting white.

Dr. Gates also suggested that "blaming the victim" is a tired excuse for the lack of progress for African Americans:

Why the huge flap over Bill Cosby's insistence that black teenagers do their homework, stay in school, master Standard English, and stop having babies? Any black person who frequents a barbershop or beauty parlor in the inner-city knows that Mr. Cosby was only echoing sentiments widely shared by the black community.

Dr. Gates's father remarked to him that, "If our people studied calculus like we studied basketball, we'd be running M.I.T."

The remarks of Mr. Barack, Dr. Gates, and Dr. Cosby ("Bill" has an Ed.D. from University of Massachusetts at Amherst), while specifically addressing the plight of poor black youth, can be readily transferred to the plight of all poor youth, no matter what their race or ethnicity. Granted, it seems that the effects of poverty particularly hurt African American kids, as fully a third of them are born into it. That said; we are relying on basketball, soccer, Little League, minimalist expectations, and the media to inculcate values on our kids, when it should be active and consistently engaging parenting that performs this task. Further, parenting should operate congruently and in unison with the schools to eradicate a pervasive pandemic of anti-intellectualism that is rampant in our country. Fifty different sets of standards and unreliable and divisive high stakes tests are adding fuel to the minimalist fires. Thinking is out of fashion.

Now is a good time to remind the reader of the remarks I made in the Foreword of this work. This book does not subscribe its contents to a buffet menu. Do all of it or none of it. That said, if the other concepts I bring up are promulgated, this one becomes easier to do.

Before you think I despise sport, I think this is also a good time to inform the reader that I am a sports fanatic. I respect the Yankees, I like the Mets, and I've been a Dodger fan since I was... well, since I was, and they played at Ebbet's Field, which was a few blocks away from where I lived in Brooklyn the first eight years of my life. I still choke up when I walk through a tunnel to my seat, as I remember my Dad taking me to my first baseball game at Ebbet's Field where the vibrant green and brown colors of the field and ultra-white player's uniforms exploded in front of me, a city kid used to shades of gray. I believe there really is a Field of Dreams in an Iowa cornfield, and I look forward to playing and watching as much baseball as I can as soon as I get this book off my chest. I believed in Babe Ruth's curse on the Red Sox and his ultimate forgiveness in 2004. In the fall, I bleed New York Jet green and white and attend Jets practice at Hofstra University, all eight home games (plus the playoffs, if we're so blessed), and if I were a few steps faster, I know in my heart that I could play free safety for them. I'll argue that Pete Rose belongs in the Hall of Fame. In March I go for the Madness. I'll follow the Knicks. I'll watch as much college and high school football as I can get. I have a poster of Coach Vince Lombardi's famous quotes in my office. It's a fantasy of mine to have lunch with Tommy Lasorda, Muhammed Ali, John Madden, Reggie Jackson, Cal

Ripken Jr., Bill Cosby, Dr. Gates, Colin Powell, Sandy Koufax, and Joe Namath. I wish Little League was eighteen kids showing up to choose up sides, getting an hour of instruction, and then playing five innings where every kids plays and their parents are reminded to mind their behaviors. Oh, yes...I'd even have the kids "ump" their own game. I like seeing little kids play soccer. I enjoy seeing kids coming out of high school locker rooms a little banged up, sweaty and exhausted, with only enough energy to eat something and get their homework done before collapsing into oblivion.

I've also been around long enough to know that sport is not going to make a better kid all by itself. As Dr. Gates reminds us in his article, only 1400 black athletes play professional baseball, football, and basketball combined, but there are 31,000 black doctors, 33,000 black lawyers, and 5,000 black dentists. The idea that a lot of black kids have that becoming a professional athlete is easier than becoming a doctor, lawyer, or dentist is obviously errant. If we consider white athletes, white kids who accede to the athletic profession in preference to all others would be at least as disappointed. Of the ten thousand or so kids I've known by working in two large school districts, I know of only six who made to major league baseball, the NFL, or the NBA. I know one Olympian. Popular as it is with kids, we don't do soccer very well as a professional sport (but keep your eye on the ladies who play it).

I know the world is crazy, and I gave you that in the opening lines of this chapter. I know this craziness forces you to work ungodly hours, sometimes at two or three jobs. I also know that in the majority of families, both parents need to work to make ends meet. I know that half of you have no help from the other half who took part in the conception of the child or children you are rearing. I know that schools need to change to accommodate your crazy life, and it's been a long time coming. This said, you must insist that your children maintain an intellectualism born of reading and dialoguing their world, and maintain a curiosity of it so that you, the parent, can guide and share in it. You need to say "no" as well as "yes." You shouldn't let your strong feelings be left as temporary manifestations of your mind. Let your child know what you are thinking, as well as the parents of those children with whom your child plays. This goes for your young children, but especially your teenagers, who are under increasing pressure to make sense of a world that is seemingly senseless at times. When you are called, and you should be called more often than when things go badly for your child, you need to come. What enraged me as a counselor and administrator was the sheer lack of interest and sensitivity (I'm going to refrain from using "brains") of parents at incredibly sensitive times in their children's lives. I went to too many funerals of kids who died from disease or horrific accidents to console some kids who had difficulty coping with the death of one of their own. What astonished me is the numbers of parents who dropped their kids off at the funeral home as if they were leaving them at a sweet sixteen party. They did not enter the room with their children where the deceased child lay in state, nor did they have the slightest interest in helping the child makes sense of what was, at the moment, a senseless outcome. Kids stayed three hours or more without any adult supervision, save a few counselors and teachers. Worse, after the doors had closed, kids waited for an hour or more for their parents to come pick them up. What was so pressing, so important at a time like this that the parent was prevented from making the time to help his or her child understand death, the most difficult thing a human endures? Worse, the parent of the deceased child had a mob of kids who didn't quite know how to react while trying to help, but making a terrible situation incredibly hard to manage.

The schools have to make room for parents to be an integral part of what they do. It's a major shortcoming of our system in use. Once that's done, schools should hold parents accountable, and not by just sending a registered letter home or a threat of the expulsion of the child. Parents who obviate their responsibilities or just "don't get it" need to be remanded to mandatory parent education and counseling, just as it would be if they were caught driving drunk. Further, the law should have big, shark-like teeth.

I'm not suggesting parents need to be put in jail (except in cases of child abuse and neglect). What I am saying is that a parent's refusal to change negative and irresponsible habits, to negate involvement in the education of the child, to ignore responsibility in child rearing, is costing us billions of dollars in providing remedial programs that only treat the child for eight or so hours a day, when the child spends the other sixteen hours at home in an environment not conducive to educational attainment. Labeling a child as having a learning dysfunction and providing special services for all or part of a school day doesn't make the child whole. While parents are currently not held at all responsible for the plight of their child, they hold a big piece of the solution in their hands. As the school discovers the depths of a child's learning dysfunction, the parent should be a major stakeholder in helping the child achieve success, rather than feeling (or allowed to play the role) like a helpless observer, or freed from any responsibility. We all have to come to realize that the words "Mom" and "Dad" are not salutations, but job titles.

College students who sign out federal student loans are forced to begin paying them back almost immediately should they terminate their education prior to the receipt of a degree. The federal government will postpone payments should the student become re-enrolled in a degree-granting program. Should the student wish to continue on to graduate school, payment of the loan is forgiven as long as the student remains enrolled. What about if we applied this concept to students who drop out of high school? They cost us a fortune in lost tax revenues, as high school dropouts have a severely limited income capacity, working "off the books" to avoid taxes, or making fewer dollars in jobs without any health or retirement benefits. Perhaps students who drop out of school should be fined a monthly sum until they become involved in programs leading to a high school diploma or its equivalency.

Currently, students who are English language learners drop out because they come to the United States as sixteen or seventeen-year-olds and have absolutely no hope of attaining a high school diploma under current course and testing requirements, which, to me, are regressive and ridiculous. Special programs for students in situations such as this need to provide alternative requirements defined for them that lead to some type of certificate of educational competency, as should students whose learning difficulties present finite expectations. For example, children with Down's syndrome or physical handicaps have enough to consume them. No matter how expensive it may be, these children deserve any service that makes their limited life span on this Earth as rich as possible. A few of the most incredible moments of my career occurred while working with handicapped children, whose gifts should not surprise anyone – you need to get beyond the disability to see them. They deserve the respect of humanity, even though their prospects may be limited. Perhaps our system should be rated by how well we take care of the weakest, for they are whom we are there to protect.

That said, kids born here should be expected to graduate. If their parents are not English speakers, they should be part of their children's educational experience so that as their child becomes literate in English, so do they. Those who immigrate should expect innovative services and educational programs that will enable their lives to be enriched and productive, and we should demand that they take advantage of them, but all the while we should respect the culture and diversity they bring to us. As importantly, we should encourage the continuity of their language. Those with limited capacities need to be educated toward their strengths rather than requiring each student to take the same courses and the same tests as if they were all going in the same direction. This realizes the obvious, that in essence we are all good at some things, and terrible at others.

For any of this to happen, new model systems need to be created. Perhaps even a new definition of what a high school diploma signifies needs to be defined. We need to redefine that word "graduate." Contextually, it may represent a vestige of expectations, not current reality. "Graduate" as a verb indicates that something follows, that some form or educational experience always awaits the graduate at another level. As it now stands, schools are still structurally and systemically geared to educate the forty percent of the population who took advantage of them 100 years ago, when a high school diploma was considered a terminal degree. Nationwide, we only graduate sixty-eight percent of our students from high school.

To me, the community college is the jewel of the country's education system. Years ago in New York State, they were advertised as "Democracy's Colleges." I don't know why they gave up that line. Indeed, they a make it possible for anyone to advance socially and educationally. They provide a plethora of programs that provide training for new careers, preparation for four-year college programs, and self-improvement. If we change the structures of K-12 education, we also must consider the community college as the great American second chance to succeed and the best vehicle to allow kids to change their minds, and provide an opportunity to society to as a whole improve their minds.

Chapter 9
National Standards Beyond NCLB

There are standards that preceded the No Child Left Behind Act (NCLB). In fact, they have been around much longer and have generated far greater impact and consequence than NCLB, so much so that one wonders why the government decided on devising its own methodology of standards and assessments. These standards represent what organizations that are vertically oriented have determined to be standards, and have undergone the scrutiny of psychometricians, teachers, college professors, high school teachers, college admission personnel, or the managers of technologically-based industries. They have proven their metal and their use is expanding at a steady rate. Colleges as well as high schools value their impact on the student preparation. They involve the constant development of staff that is responsible for their execution. Students find involvement in them incredibly powerful, as they can mean jobs, college admission, scholarships, advanced standing in college, and a chance to test their metal against their peers nationwide. They also allow students to exercise their intentionalilty, as their active participation through dialogue and the social construction of knowledge is part and parcel to the expectation of success. They represent choice, not mandates, and reflect the opportunity to construct truth through dialogic and experiential means as opposed to accepting truth of what others have unilaterally judged to be relevant and mandatory. They also embody futuristic opportunity as opposed to the past and present states of mandated compliance that standards-based reform and its accompanying high stakes assessments have come to represent.

I like the SAT. Perhaps you are already thinking that I have aligned myself with the devil for saying this. I haven't. In fact, I think I'm in good company. An overwhelming majority of college admissions officials stand by the SAT as a measure that levels the playing field for students. Consider the thousands of high schools in the United States, each with their own curricula that is now influenced by the standards and assessments the individual states have concocted to meet the requirements of NCLB. Also consider that each high school has its own internal politics that determines grades students receive. Add to this the wild swings between the have and have-not school districts and multicultural, ethnic, and other social factors that the influence learning experiences provided to the kids. Bring all of this to the college admissions table and you have an incredible array of credentials to sort and evaluate in order to make an admissions decision. What the SAT does is provide a measure to aid in this evaluation.

The SAT was first introduced in 1926 as a means for the Ivy League colleges to assess the growing number of applicants. The population of the United States back then was approximately 117 million, with 941,000 individuals enrolled in college. Changes in the structure of the SAT for the Spring 2005 administration include the addition of a writing sample, an end to analogies, and questions in mathematics more in line with high school curriculum. At this time, the numbers of students enrolled in higher education has increased to 14.2 million with the nation's population swelling to 260 million.

Some say the SAT is prejudicial. The exam itself is not, but it invariably shows that poor kids and kids who are minorities struggle more than their white counterparts because the social and economic capital they bring to their testing centers is not what the white majority of SAT takers bring. The College Board, the owners of the SAT, has used the test to voice concern to this inequity, and has provided leadership in bringing to the public discourse the intrinsic value of equity in education. This action has made a difference. While gaps still exist, they are narrowing.

Those who criticize the SAT or profit from a variety of test preparation or college counseling programs would have you believe that only students who score in the lofty 1300+ range will have the opportunity to attend college. It seems that most literature on colleges from sources other than the college admissions offices would lead some individuals to believe this is the case. This is nonsense. What test preparation provides is a means to allay pressure by familiarizing the student with the exam's format and drill on sample testing questions. In this way, the "fear factor" is neutralized and the student becomes alerted to possible questions and situations still requiring critical thought for a solution. Nonetheless, after doing college admission work for more than thirty years, I still say there is a college for everyone, and everyone should maintain the option to attend college, regardless of the SAT score. What we need to do to make this statement more realistic and widespread is to provide a better means of conveying information so it reaches the most desperate kids and families through the offices of the high school. SAT scores will rise if those who know little about the college selection process become informed of the possibilities—when a goal is set, the road to it becomes more conceivable and plausible. The number of students who take the SAT and the scores that they achieve in part measures high school effectiveness. The College Board will agree that more than the score, the numbers of students who take the SAT is a better measure of the high school's intent to provide a first step to equity and excellence for their students.

One more thing about the SAT: it was designed from its start seventy-eight years ago to provide colleges with a measure of how well students would do in their first year of college. It was not intended as a scholarship exam or an instrument that could be used to determine how students are chosen for gifted and talented programs or honors status in a variety of venues. While the SAT is used for these purposes, it was not specifically designed for them. It stands as a measure of how equitable our society is in administering education to our youth, and making alternatives for the future more possible.

The SAT is only one measure that helps students determine the selectivity of the colleges to which they can apply. Grades, challenging coursework, leadership in community and school activities, letters of recommendation, and a sincere interest in the kind of educational experience a college offers are equal or more important than an SAT score, predicated on the college. Students with perfect SAT scores (800 Verbal, 800 Math) are not at all guaranteed acceptance to the country's most selective colleges. The SAT score should be complementary to the degree of success a student has achieved in taking his or her high school's most rigorous coursework. In many instances, Advanced Placement, or what is more commonly referred to as "AP," represents this rigor.

AP began in the 1955-56 academic year, with 1,229 students from 104 high schools taking 2,199 AP exams. The program since then has grown exponentially, with 1,101,802 students representing more than 14,000 high schools taking 1,887,770 AP Exams. The program was initially intended to offer high school students the opportunity to take college level coursework, and an AP test score of three, four, or five on a scale of one to five would buy a student college credit. The student did not have to take the freshman level course, and thus would save tuition dollars. Since then, the competitiveness of students and the academic excellence of high schools have come to be measured by the numbers of students who take AP, the numbers of AP courses offered, and the scores students attain. I would offer that AP is fast becoming more of a standard of selectivity than the SAT, as it is the nation's only high school curriculum in widespread use. Students are taught the same curricula and are prepared to take the same tests across the nation.

The AP program really "brings it" in the educational context. The various curricula in art, math, science, English, social studies, and languages other than English are written by high school teachers and college faculty, as are the yearly assessments offered each spring. Teachers are offered a wide range of staff development activities through The College Board. Communication between The College Board's AP office and schools is efficient and effective. Educational institutions and the media alike tout the value of the program. State legislatures and the Congress have recognized the importance of AP by providing or supplementing testing fees for students who cannot afford to take the exams. If there is an educational success story of challenging kids and teachers to reach higher, it is the story of AP. Movies have been made about its effect, most notably Stand and Deliver, its subject the work of AP Calculus teacher Jaime Escalante in turning around a trouble-ridden Los Angeles high school that served mostly minority kids. The story is inspiring, and its theme is repeated yearly in schools across the nation.

The International Baccalaureate (IB) is yet another example of a national standard that "brings it." Though not as universal as AP, the program grows yearly. IB was founded by the visionary educator Alec Peterson as a part of the offerings of the United World Colleges (UWC), a chain of international schools providing youngsters worldwide the opportunity to live and learn together. The IB is a college entrance assessment that can be taken in any country and is recognized by colleges internationally. The IB program and the UWC colleges have experienced tremendous growth since their establishment in the 1960s, and are gaining increasing recognition almost everywhere for unique educational opportunities and excellence. There are now over 1200 IB schools worldwide, and the numbers of IB schools in the United States is growing faster than anywhere else in the world.

The IB Diploma Programme is a comprehensive two-year curriculum and assessment system that requires students to study courses across all disciplines. Within this structured framework, the Diploma Programme provides a great deal of flexibility, accommodating student interest and abilities. Through careful subject selection, students may tailor their course of study to meet their needs. Regardless of the subject selection, all students will "explore the connections between the six major subject areas, will study each subject through an international perspective, will reflect critically on what it means to be a knower, will pursue one subject in great detail through independent research, and will have the opportunity to apply their knowledge and skills in local and community outreach." Assessment is carried out in a variety of ways through the course of the two-year program, including assessment by outside examiners as well as the student's teachers. It is based on an international standard applied worldwide.

What is it about these programs that bring out the student in the kid and teacher in the instructor? Philosophers would indicate that they are the source of true learning and are synchronous and congruent to our nature as human beings. In short, we learn best what we choose to learn, and we choose what we want to learn to satisfy our curiosity or complement our talents. We like to talk to others about these things, we like to show off our accomplishments, and we feel accomplished when we conquer a challenge that shows our collective stuff. The test as a stand-alone assessment of knowledge does not come near to doing this. Our penchant to want to measure everything and anything causes us to come to a destination without experiencing the joy of the journey. Consider the following.

Research has shown that high school students see more value in those educational systems and structures left untouched by standards-based reform, specifically the extracurriculum, opportunities for experiential learning, and elective courses that now fall mostly under the purview of seniors, as the mandates for required courses have displaced them in the earlier high school years. Programs like Advanced Placement and IB, though vigorous and demanding, are seen as a choice made by students with a connection to their futures, as more and more students participate in them every year. They relish the small learning communities indirectly created by the fame and recognition IB and AP have attained with school districts. How does this fit in with standards-based reform and high stakes tests? With standards and assessments, we are dealing with a mandatory, solitary accomplishment in a minimal and narrowed experience, and we assess it through a mandatory high stakes test. With AP and IB, there is no mandate. Students choose to be in these programs. Critical thinking and social construction provided by generally smaller classes of students who have also elected participation mark educational methods and body of instruction of these programs.

The Tech Prep program was a national endeavor to provide the individuals needed to address the wide range and ever-growing technology needs of the nation through an applied-based curriculum, though it has barely survived the quantitative wrath of NCLB. Tech Prep provided students with a challenging course of study in high school that would be complemented by a continuity of training at a two-year college or technical school. High schools and colleges signed agreements to allow students a "seamless transition" where no coursework would be duplicated. Specialized English courses were created to teach students skills specific to the course of study the student would pursue. There were also provisions for students to attend four-year programs immediately from high school, or after completing a two-year community college program. Kids loved Tech Prep. It was seen as reality-based education, with the opportunity to constantly challenge and create new mastery as the technological knowledge base expanded.

The extracurriculum is where kids flourish. They choose their participation, and they work feverishly at achieving excellence. Take a look at the school's athletic program. Kids stay late and wear themselves out after grueling practices or highly competitive games, meets, or matches. They are bruised and battered, and yet they come day after day. Kids in school plays rehearse well into the night. They, like their athlete counterparts, understand that the authentic assessment they endure is the most grueling of all ordeals. They live for the applause and work with each other tirelessly to succeed. Their coaches and directors are mentors, working side by side with them in turning a love into a socially constructed success story. The USA FIRST Robotics competition has caught fire nationally because kids and their teachers chose to participate in the almost impossible task of building a working robot to fulfill a specific function within two weeks from a box of sophisticated spare parts, then shipping it off to a competition where genius is on display. I have known kids and teachers working over weekends, vacation periods, and through the night to make a deadline, and they do it happily. They value each other's opinions, experientially trial and error their thoughts, and have confidence in their final product. More so, they learn to trust each other and respect their individual abilities.

What do all of these kids have in common? Simply, to be the best as determined by incredible authentic competitions to achieve excellence. You don't get that from one exam of a narrowed course of study deemed to make the recipient "competent." If anything, competency in this sense is then a compromise.

Let me explain. It appears that the self-starting directional control of students' consciousness has dealt with the issue of standards-based reform and high stakes assessment as well as their accompanying failing systems and structures by creating a duality:

Those things students identified as empowering their learning; that is, the issue of students' intentionality is more associated with active learning where choice, experiential possibilities, and smaller, more intimate learning structures are operationalized, empower teacher agency, and provide opportunities for authentic assessment and socially constructed learning experiences during ample opportunities to dialogue.

Those issues that students feel defeat their learning that are mired in systems that are regressive and impersonal, and curriculum and methods narrowed to tests whose meaning vanishes upon the student's response to the last question on any particular state-level test. Students have extreme distaste to educational experiences without dialogue that force them into a passive role devoid of any social construction.

In terms of meaning assigned by the student, the more standards and high stakes assessments are imposed that result in reduced opportunities for experiential activities and dialogue, the less actual student control can be exercised; attempts at control are mediated by the self-starting directional control (the human ability of making a choice) of the student. Hence, if not recognized as such by the student, no standard, either legislated or imagined, actually exists beyond minimal compliance.

The duality of consciousness has forced a mitigation of the student's intentionality between the passive subjectivity perceived to be imposed by standards-based reform with the active objectivity that is marked by experiential learning, dialogue, and the social construction of knowledge. Though a matter of degree and not absolute, the words passive and active tell a story from the point of view of learning's temporal possibilities. Passivity connotes a limited engagement with a present-tense experience based on a body of knowledge that has already been discovered, packaged, and closed to discussion. It is deemed as undeniable truth. Activity indicates a present-tense engagement whose future outcome is open to a variety of possibilities. Here, the search for truth continues into the future in terms of discovering possibilities and meanings. The excitement of not knowing how "all of this" will turn out appears to keep students engaged and committed to socially constructed outcomes They feel they are needed and their work is appreciated, especially if enhanced by experiential opportunities. It's why kids like roller coasters – what lies beyond the next turn or uptake is unknown, but yet the discovery is exhilarating. It provides a new, tried and true definition of the phrase I know.

The more active learning becomes, the more the implications that the search for truth temporally continues into the future in terms of discovering possibilities and meanings. Think historically about this—any historical discovery that was noted as having had extraordinary consequence began with a question arising from an individual or small group of dialoguing intentional individuals questioning an accepted paradigm. Newton and Galileo asked these questions, as did Jefferson and Adams. They made clear the example that when the concepts of thought are free to use their ability to question and discover, dramatic change can occur. Standards-based reform interprets that questions (or assessments) are to be confined to what has been narrowly established as truth. The human desire to establish knowledge through social construction or dialogue, therefore, is summarily dismissed by standards-based reform—what it demands of students is to know only what has been defined by others as having established value as knowledge. Thus narrowed, established knowledge is carried over into the present. Its accompanying assessments allegedly demonstrate the percentage of mastery. While the state passively denies the students' ability to question and form knowledge, students' ability to question and form knowledge actively denies the state's standards-based meaning of truth. Thus, it appears that the question, "Whaddya think?" (here expressed in my native Brooklynese to simplify its meaning) seems not to have been asked. This is a tragedy.

The duality of mitigating consciousness can be further exemplified by the demand of standards-based reform through its assessments in the regular curriculum, and the desire to learn in the extracurriculum. Student intentionality skirmishes with standards-based demands, handling them in the most efficient and non-engaging means. Again, though not absolute and a matter of degree, it flourishes when its desires are actualized in practice. A demand is a present tense issue. It needs to be addressed directly by the consciousness through action, negotiation, or perhaps it is ignored. While the consequences may prove to be dire in miscalculating or underestimating a standards-based demand, a student's consciousness interprets it as a present tense issue whose importance will not be elevated even with a positive solution or outcome, as it still will not improve the student's ability to know and learn beyond the engagement of the demand. It is not a problem to be solved, but a needful thing that requires attention, in that dialogue is not required to address it, to socially construct meaning from it. The standards-based demand is an issue of "I am," as students are assessed and judged individually. There is no application to the future, just a demand of the present based the truth as it was established in the past by others. There is no competition, no construction, just submission to a power that does not recognize the humanity of thought.

On the other hand, a desire recognizes the conscious drive to know and postulates that learning is motivated by this human need to acquire knowledge (the word conscious is derived from the Latin, loosely meaning "to be aware of "). The temporality associated with desire sees the present as the temporal place to begin to question a pre-established truth. Desire views time as a function of this motivation to learn, quite the opposite of a demand. The demands of standards-based reform predicate the narrowing of knowledge where success is judged through a one-time assessment without dialogue, and no chance learn with others by experiential trial and error. The desires of the consciousness predicate that success is a goal achieved through constant learning and relearning, a cyclic loop of reinforcing action through dialogue, where the past serves as prologue. The established truth of the past is re-examined through dialogue in the present to construct knowledge socially for application in the future. If assessment is driving standards and standards are narrowed to linearly testable outcomes, learning in the real sense becomes secondary.

I refer to the work of Jurgen Habermas, who offered the Theory of Communicative Action, a philosophy of analysis and action based on the human ability to communicate intent, with an analysis of dialogue that serves to provide an analytic means as to how Heidegger's individual beings create societies that create systems, all of which are interdependent. Through symbolic interaction, we reach for understanding when we justify, convince, defend, criticize, explain, argue, or express our inner feelings and desires while we interpret those of others. The task of communicative action is to study rationally the legitimacy of a norm to find the good reasons that cause its acceptance, so as to produce norms that are in the general interest as well as norms that are recognized to be in the general interest.

Habermas argued that political institutions couldn't be maintained through strategic manipulation, such as the mandates placed on schools by standards-based reform. Although the threat of sanctions or rewards is part of the motivation to adhere to mandates, they cannot guarantee mass loyalty. While elected to serve by the populace, Habermas offers that legislative focus becomes a contrived concept centered on legality, not a result of dialogue with the people it was meant to serve. Stability requires that reasons for obedience must be mobilized and justified in the eyes of those concerned. If not, the gain in control is paid for with a loss of meaning. The complete denial of the students' intentionality coupled with the fact that there was no dialogue between them or their teacher-agents and the legislative will of the state made the issue contentious from the start.

It is difficult to argue the concept of high standards. Who would deny that we want the absolute best for and from our children? This begs a second question—by what means should they be implemented? The present means of severe sanctions brought about by high stakes assessments result in narrowing the effort so as to negate its true intent. While recognized as a norm, research has shown that what has resulted is a tacit dismissal of not only the premise of standards-based reform, but its execution as well by the students it was meant to serve. The legislated demand to quantify what was learned limited what could be taught and the manner it which it is put forth. To students, the high stakes, assessment-driven, standards-based curriculum is an invalid attack on their intentionality as noted by their favor of the experiential and extracurricular possibilities open to them.

Habermas sought to create a systems theory by rooting it in the perspectives and meanings individuals make of learning and how they dialogue these perspectives to construct knowledge socially, much as Peter Senge has done with his book, *The Fifth Discipline*. Rather than seeking to explore behavioral response, Peter Senge offered a critical methodology for solutions based on the idea that organizations work the way they do because of how the individuals in the organizations think and interact. To present the systemic perspective, I offer a review of Senge's major points.

As presented in his books *The Fifth Discipline* and *Schools That Learn*, Senge's integrated systems theory of the learning organization is centered on what he refers to as five disciplines, which include systems thinking, shared vision, mental models, team learning, and personal mastery. Echoing the philosophers, Senge determined that the disciplines center on dialogue, a free-flowing social construction of meaning by which one can view his or her thinking. Like Habermas, Senge associates the organization's ability to recreate itself through socially constructed learning and, in doing so, to re-perceive the world to create the future. One would think that schools would be the ultimate learning organizations, as students give us the opportunity to re-perceive the world through the natality they bring to us, and thus act as the stimulus to re-create our systems and structures constantly. However, regressive structures, systems, and practices are perceived as negating the objective "real world" needs in order to satisfy a legislated quantification of the subjective "as is" of the current high school. Standards-based assessments intensified the bad practices of passive rote-based acceptance of narrowed truth-as-legislated.

As viewed by Senge's principles, what standards-based reform fails to realize is that the system fosters its own behavior, and disregards that the behaviors demonstrated—by all involved in the school community—reflect problems that were built over time. State and federal officials' enthusiastic demands for cheap, instantaneous fixes through standards-based reform fall short, as the problems are more than an academic foundering that can be fixed by rigid curriculum and tests. Students' perceptions are dismissed, or not even sought, while the decisions made further from the ultimate evaluator (in this case the student) will make the collapse only more dramatic. Without a disciplined systems approach to reform, what Senge identified as compensating feedback comes into play—the harder the system is pushed, the harder it pushes back. Schools have retrenched themselves into stale, systemic structures with standards-based reform, quite the opposite of reform's intent. As Senge wrote:

Pushing harder and harder and harder on familiar solutions while fundamental problems persist or worsen is a reliable indicator of non-systemic thinking—what we often call the "what we need is a bigger hammer" syndrome. (*The Fifth Discipline*, p. 62).

The whole of the linear standards-based system is driven by assessment and not as a means to meet the needs of students. It provides students no meaningful feedback, other than a grade that fails to reinforce meaning or assess mastery. Students find their intentional needs met by the integrated structures and systems that standards-based reform has ignored as extraneous in scope and sequence to education. As Senge might explain it, they have identified an economy of means, whereby those structures that are valued are negligible in cost when compared to the huge investments made by the current standards-based structures and systems to perpetuate themselves. Those structures, though negligible in cost, are incredibly important to students even though their assessment is authentic, sometimes painful, but nonetheless has meaning that is highly valued. It is akin to buying a child a very expensive toy, then watching the child play in the box the toy came in, letting the mind's possibilities and imagination run beyond the toy's limited, pre-determined structural and performance envelopes. This results in what Senge defines as leverage, which is constituted by minute changes in structure leading to significant and enduring improvements, despite the existing system. Interviews I conducted with high school seniors and recent alums as part of my dissertation indicated that what they fondly recalled were the details of those experiential and extracurricular involvements and Advanced Placement. They thought of their high stakes Regents exams as terminal in feedback, shortsighted in scope, and insignificant to

consequence. Their connections to "the real world" were unseen
or unrecognized by students.

Senge's discipline of personal mastery may be employed to describe the students' vision (to extend to the self-defined meaning of
intentionality) developed through their experiential and extracurricular involvement, using their current reality as a sail rather than
an anchor. They found structures where they were a part of a larger
creative process and yet could maintain their uniqueness. They
want those conditions because their mind's learning processes tell
them they do. Personal mastery cannot be measured by standards
or criteria. No one will ever be able to measure to three decimal
places how much personal mastery contributes to productivity
and the bottom line As Senge noted, without intentionality; excellence becomes another "buzz word."

The duality resulting from standards-based reform and its artificial and formalistic dependencies as opposed to the intentionally
authentic and internalized opportunities students see as all-impor-
tant is plainly evident by examining personal mastery. It is unique
to schools that while not supported by nearly comparative expenditures to the regular curriculum, the extracurriculum is used to
portray the school as an organization that is supportive of student
personal mastery, making much ado about student theatrical pro-
ductions, success in sports programs, and contests that students
enter as not-for-credit volunteers. While recognizing the value of
its outcomes, schools maintain rigidity in the regular curriculum
that does not embrace the notion of personal mastery. Students
committed to personal mastery through competitive, authentic assessment, or in experiential and extracurricular avenues, persevere,
even though they experienced frustrations with standards-based
structures and systems. As Senge noted:

Competition is one of the best structures yet invented by hu-
mankind to allow each of us to bring out the best in each other.
But after the competition is over...it's one's sense of purpose that
draws you further...This is why personal mastery is a process of
continually re-focusing on what one truly wants (*The Fifth Discipline*, p.149).

Personal mastery becomes a shared vision when a task is en-
countered or a challenge is made. Those who share their thoughts
and their thinking to a common cause become identified with it,
almost inseparable from it. How students viewed the extracurriculum and the energy they and their teachers put forth in achieving
a goal is evidence of this. Long hours, continuous authentic assessment, and constant dialogue became the basis for a culture of
must-do. If schools are to be classified as learning organizations,
the participants in the organization need to develop a shared vi-

sion. As my informants related, this happens in the extracurriculum. With shared vision, Senge ventured:

The task was no longer separate from the self...but rather he (sic) identified with this task so strongly that you couldn't define his real self without including that task (*The Fifth Discipline*, p. 208).

At the USA FIRST Robotics competitions I attended, teams of students had tee shirts, hats, and jackets with "Robot Man -'03" printed above a picture of the quintessential Robbie the Robot. One robotics team from the Bronx, New York had "Ghetto-Techs" on their shirts. These students exposed their ways of thinking to recognize organizational shortcomings that would prevent their shared visions from achieving the level of mastery and assessment they did—their tee-shirts literally, "we are here, together, despite the negativity of organizationally produced labels." Their vision was locally developed, not a pre-packaged interpretation truth. It was arrived at by dialogue. It was not just a solution to a problem, but a socially constructed united exercise in "what can be." Students through the extracurriculum build a "real world" that is a microcosm of a learning organization within a standards-based, tightly controlled, yet dysfunctional structure that marginalized them. The school-as-organization does not mock it, though—pictures of kids doing "their thing," winning games, displaying a love of an art mastered or a musical instrument's literal extension of their minds and bodies, and reveling in each other's competitive, problem-solving company—those are the things that get school budgets passed and kids into Harvard.

As Senge may surmise, while students displayed enrollment in the regular curricular program with various levels of compliance, they are not committed. It's like ham and eggs – the chicken in compliant but the pig is committed. I venture that kids would agree that school is necessary, but their level of compliance in the regular educational structure and system may drift between none and substantive, with state-sponsored high stakes tests being somewhat middle ground, and Advanced Placement holding the highest degree of esteem within this context. It is in the extracurriculum and its experiential possibilities where they show commitment, where they will do whatever it takes to make the vision real. I surmise that where the school-as-organization is actually learning, it is through the experiential shared vision created by teachers and students in the extracurriculum.

In the context of this line of reasoning, it is interesting to note that a study recently conducted at Ball State University found that those states who employ high stakes exit exams to certify students for graduation have SAT scores thirty points lower than those states without exit exams. A study conducted at the University of Oregon's Center for Policy Research also state that administered exams are inconsistent in demonstrating preparation for college in critical thinking skills and writing. The state exams are achievement-based and aimed at specific content knowledge, whereas the SAT is based upon a student's ability to reason through complex problems. At this same juncture, the September 1, 2004 edition of *Education Week* reported that New Hampshire is considering loosening up state standards "so that students can apply real world learning experiences toward their diplomas and use assessments to bypass more of their traditional course work." Based upon the offerings of this chapter, I'll let the reader draw his or her own conclusions about educational efficacy as it pertains to these two specific issues.

With standards-based reform, it is the old story that's told about the dean who gets in front of a class of incoming freshmen and tells them, "Look to the right of you and to the left of you. One of you won't be here come the spring." That's an old-style threat that is an empty parody for organizational failure pinned on the student. In the extracurriculum, Tech Prep, AP, and the IB, it is more like, "Look to the right of you and to the left of you. Those are the people who will get you through." Odd as it may seem, the latter is how the most elite Army units and the Marines work, which consider it dishonor to leave anyone behind.

Chapter 10
The Institution of The Board of Education—A Vestige of Simpler Times

The institution of the Board of Education has a long history in the United States, and is unique to this nation. No other industrialized nation places so much emphasis on the local control of the educational process. The model for the school board dates back to colonial New England where in 1647 the legislature of Massachusetts required towns to foster and monitor the education of their children. As towns expanded, direct popular control of the schools became difficult, so local boards were elected to govern the schools that grew in size and number as their towns did. As the country expanded past the Ohio River, the New England model became transported to the west as an efficient means of school governance.

Communities elect school board trustees as their representatives, and as trustees they have fiduciary powers ascribed to them by state Education Departments and legislatures. Board members are to promote education as a public interest while at the same time upholding the values and cultures of the community that elected them. They also are the stewards of the district's finances.

In terms of personnel, school boards hire and fire teachers, principals, and superintendents of schools as well as custodians, clerks, secretaries and anyone who receives compensation from the school district for services performed. They approve the competitive bids of the construction companies to build or fix schools, as well as companies who install phones, computers, provide lunches to children, and a plethora of other functions. They also build budgets, set tax rates, and approve expenditures. All of this relies upon the recommendations of the district's administrative staff, particularly the superintendent of schools.

In terms of policy, the school board reflects the community's will, hears citizens who feel a policy or the personnel who implement it have somehow wronged them, and remains vigilant as to the growth of the school's academic and extracurricular programs.

As with any elected official or body, school boards are political entities. As noted by Keith Goldhammer in his 1964 book *The School Board*, a number of studies discovered that school board members were more dedicated to the status quo than innovation, or felt their jobs were political patronage posts they were elected to in order to represent a special interest. He quotes researcher Neal Gross in saying that school board members had hazy notions of their jobs and spent considerable time dealing in trivialities:

Some school board members act as if they, as individuals, had the right to make decisions, which is the prerogative of the entire school board. Some school board members act as if they, rather than the superintendent, had the right to administer the policy decisions of the board (p. 37).

In economically tough times, individuals are elected to boards of education who promise to "cut wasteful spending," cut the salaries of teachers whom their constituency feel are paid too much, and thin the administrative ranks. Fluctuations in the national economy and political pandering in the state legislatures spell fiscal disasters for schools, especially when "get tough" board members are elected by promising not to cut any programs, but cut spending. This is fiscally impossible let alone irresponsible. It is emotionalism replacing reasoning, and political carpet bagging replacing solid management. It is a myopic attempt to reign in a system that outraged trustee candidates have sold to the voters as fiscally out of control and educationally malfeasant. This is not a new occurrence.

The reader might remember the name James B. Conant from Chapter 5. Among his recommendations for creating larger high schools in his book *The American High School*, Conant related that the first essential ingredient for a good high school is:

...A school board composed of intelligent, understanding citizens who realize fully the distinction between policy making and administration.

Unfortunately, this is not the case in too many instances. In fact, the bigger the school district, the more disparate and dangerous this issue becomes, as board members either seek broad support for increasing their power over administration, or become the instruments of constituent groups in the community who lobby to sway decisions, however unsound, in their direction. Mostly, it's about money.

Since colonial times, the issue of taxation has been sounded over and again as a predominant issue in any election, as it is now in the 2004 presidential race that predominates the nation's attention as I write this book. It is also the same issue that politicians use as the biggest sucker punch they throw at the voting public. School board candidates, local town and county candidates, as well as the candidates for state offices promise to lower taxes as much as federal officials. What the public is slow to recognize is that taxes indeed can be cut, but along with the cut comes a commensurate reduction in the services government, including school boards, may provide.

A "tax revolt" at the state level enacts cuts that local county and town governments feel the necessity to cover with increased sales taxes, user fees, and property taxes, as commensurate cuts in services are locally unthinkable—the farther away the decisions for taxation and program reductions are made, the less the impact of the outcomes of such actions are felt. To give an example of this dysfunction, I use a story from the Vietnam War, the ultimate dysfunction. The helicopter became the new "Jeep" for the battalion or regimental commander in Vietnam. Many of these aircraft returned to their bases bullet-ridden. When the holes were measured, military officials were startled to find that it was American bullets that made them, not Communist weapons. It was determined that the decisions made literally "on high" were devoid of the immediate input of the screams of the wounded and dying, and that those on the ground wanted those in the air to know how they felt. In a gubernatorial election in New Jersey, Christy Todd Whitman's overwhelming victory was marked by keeping her promise to slash spending and taxes at the state level, which was applauded by everyone in the state. The next year local property taxes skyrocketed to compensate for the cuts in state spending and taxation. These taxes pay for county and town services and programs that local politicians, to include school board members, felt were important to maintain as they are closer to their end-user constituents. In the company of school aid that emanates from the state legislature based upon complicated and obsolescent formulas, local taxes enhance the operating expenditures for the local school districts. To the chagrin of the local homeowner, local taxes are raised to offset the declining revenue from the state. So while state taxes may be reduced somewhat, local taxes rise more sharply, so much so that the raise in taxes locally exceeds the cut in taxes at the state level—the state can tax more individuals and its taxes are therefore not as drastically raised; and locally, the formulas used to assess property taxes are inequitable and out-of-date. The natural reaction is to blame the local officials for their malfeasance. The school districts are particularly vulnerable, as the tax-setting body is the locally elected school board. Thus, "non-mandated" programs are put on the chopping block, such as music, art, bus transportation limits, full-day kindergarten, counseling services, athletics, and school lunches. To cut personnel, who make up the bulk of a district's expenditures, class sizes will be raised, non-classroom staff trimmed, custodial staff cut, and administrative staff reduced. All of these are painful choices, as the educational and practical consequences are usually, but not always, considered more dire than the school board raising local property taxes.

When locals discover that most of a district's expenditures are unfunded but mandated programs by the state or federal education bureaus and legislatures, the sucker punch becomes a roundhouse right. Lashing out at the state capitol may be difficult, but the school board meets locally twice monthly. You can almost hear the referee counting to ten to signify the knockout.

Even though school board members are not paid for their service, they nonetheless become quite enamored with the power, however minimal, they have gained. Getting re-elected becomes a priority over doing the right thing. This leads to the outcomes that Goldhammer summarized way back in 1964:

As long as local control leads to local irresponsibility with respect to the provision of the resources needed to maintain the quality of education, the critics of local control will find many examples of how communities fail to bear their responsibilities for promoting the national interest.

And:

As long as school boards place parochial interests before national needs and the requirements of the broader society, local control imposes a barrier to both the proper defense and the full development of society (p.109).

This is especially so in big school districts, where residents are not represented accordingly due to the relatively small size (five, seven, or nine members) of their school boards. In smaller districts, school boards seem to work as the New England model may have intended. They are not as dependent on state aid, their population growth is limited by their more defined boundaries, curriculum and teacher performance is more easily monitored, and they generally serve an educationally and culturally sophisticated population that has an intrinsic knowledge of the entire educational process through the college level. Small populations are represented well by school boards, although school districts with little wealth may in fact be in the same situation as large school districts. Minority districts are especially hard hit by the inadequacy of local and state funding formulas that are highly inequitable. Boards of education in these instances become the worst kind of political entities, as the decisions they make are based on inadequate dollars, unsubstantiated assumptions, and general ignorance of the opportunities and operations of schools, not the relative inadequacy of the educational experience for their children.

The antithesis to proper representative control is the large school district. On Long Island, where there are many large school districts (6000+ students), I have been witness to a board member demanding and sustaining the termination of an administrator because she complained about giving special treatment to the board member's teacher-son who wanted a special set of report cards run for him. Another board decided not to give teachers tenure just because they simply did not believe in it, despite the fact the process of its award was legislated and the law. In another instance, running on a platform that strove to reduce costs in a district already struggling fiscally from year to year, the district was nearly bankrupt by a "tax pac" school board. Due to economic recession, state funding in an era of new state mandates and a commensurate increase in staff and other expenditures was cut dramatically. What brought out these educational revolutionaries (as they liked to be viewed) was the issue that just to maintain programs, the tax rate increase was proposed at over twenty-five percent. A rather nonsophisticated public that overwhelmingly elected them did not see through the problem and instead sought revenge at the local level for difficulties that arose at the national and state levels. Programs did not grow with the needs of students; others of promise were cut altogether. Staff in non-instructional areas and special services was not replaced upon retirement, even though the district's student population was growing and state and federal mandated demands were increasing the workloads. Because the district's tax rate was among the lowest on Long Island, poor families whose children had specific remedial needs entered the district as a place they could afford to live. This new population included a burgeoning population of children for whom English is not the primary language spoken at home. A student population with promise but lacking in economic capital was left to founder in terms of seeking higher education. Attracting and maintaining qualified staff for a variety of positions became difficult, but the board felt obligated nonetheless to return a $1.00 rebate to each taxpayer to show their resolve in cutting costs.

One would think that individuals who run for the board of education would have enough of a vested interest in the process of education to raise their own children, yet this is not a requirement for board membership, which makes one wonder about the motivation these individuals have. Surely there are other political offices one could seek where responsibilities are not defined as close to the specific purpose of the education of a community's children. One is also tempted to look at the educational level of board of education members as a means of determining their ability to make informed and logical decisions, but this does not correlate. Individuals who are high school graduates and working for the post office as well as those with graduate degrees have made incredibly and profoundly poor decisions based solely on their corruption of power, their twisted interpretation of state mandates, or their crusade to cut taxes. Yet others from all walks of life, even high school dropouts, have been selfless and reflective in managing school districts.

To defeat incumbents, teacher unions and candidates make back-door deals with community groups. This causes more political upheaval in the long term, and spawns administrative management difficulties in the short term. Those who attain power feel their primary mission is to punish those who lost it. In these ludicrous wars, education and children become casualties.

The question becomes: How much more immersed in politics do children have to be in order to be immersed in an equitable and sound educational process?

Should boards of education be done away with? I think not, as they are a vehicle for the community to voice its collective and individual educational concern for its children. But there needs to be a rethinking of their purposes and the margins of their actions through a reorganization of their duties and a clearly defined set of parameters of their responsibilities. The present fine line between creating and executing policy dividing boards of education and the administrators that they hire has been crossed time and again. What facilitates and fuels this errant occurrence is that we as a nation have no specific national educational goals, and states are pursuing fifty different paths to achieving the dubious demands of NCLB, meaning that local boards may be making horrendous decisions. Another layer of politically charged laymen deciding the country's future, especially in big suburban and city school districts, is clearly and simply not in the national interest, to say nothing of the interest of children. Though I feel it a terrible misstep with the best of intentions, one of the reasons the federal government stormed in with NCLB was because of the educational inequities manifested in part due to the ineffectiveness of state and local entities in providing "world class educational standards" for all children. Though it left it up to the states as to how they were going to comply with the mandates based mostly on assessment, with NCLB the federal government created a precedent at defining educational reform at the national level, however loosely, though institutions and traditions such as boards of education were not at all effected in their operations, just as the archaic structures and systems of the public schools was left intact. Education became a hot political topic as a result. Because of this, it is my thinking that the next round of reform after NCLB will also originate at the national level, but will be even more dramatic in its specificity. Other things will change as well, but the mandate of the board of education will surely be evaluated with a most discerning eye. Our place in the global community of nations cannot be left up to institutions and individuals who fail to realize the true depth of responsibility of their charge. You cannot get ahead if the mission or your particular penchant is to get even, or worse, regression.

The problems of local control stem from the idea that everyone thinks they know about education because they went to school, a construct already mentioned in this book. The layman has no idea how complicated the school as an organization can be. Board members are totally unprepared for the scope, sequence, and depth of the problems they will deal with. Instead of becoming learners, they revert to the imprints of the negativity that got them elected, however simplistic or twisted those ideas are. Their first charge is to listen and learn, not think. Yet, they cast votes on vital issues without any knowledge or firsthand experience of the impact of that vote. Remember my Vietnam helicopter metaphor? How much further from the activities in the classroom can a board of education be? Superintendents themselves in large districts are too removed by what their jobs have become, and boards of education rely on them specifically to keep them informed. The data upon which superintendents make decisions may not be valid or reliable, depending on how close to the action the superintendent's staff that creates them resides on the district's personnel chart. Should boards be data gatherers? Their legal charge says they should be. Are they? Probably not, and they will not be as long as the political face rules their existence and overshadows the totality of their fiduciary responsibilities. Simply put, they will not be trusted.

Yale University educator Seymour Sarason indicated in his 1994 book *Parental Involvement* and the *Political Principal* that learning must arise from a forum where the participants can freely exchange ideas without penalty, that in fact this is a political right, no matter how unpopular the views presented are. Forums of teachers, administrators, and board members are a first step in this direction. However, the one postulate of such forums is that the organization-institution as it is, to include everything about the operations of schools, gives rise to far more problems than it solves. Schools as institutions are status-quo aficionados—they resist change and the inquiries between the layers of administrators, teachers, and board of education members that might promote it. As a result, boards of education are part of the problem, not the solution.

To replace the board of education, Sarason endorses the idea of the Educational Assembly, first proposed by researchers John Henry Martin and Charles Harrison in their 1972 book, *Free to Learn*. The establishment of voting districts for education across a city or large school district would create the Assembly; and each district would send representatives to this new legislative body. The Assembly would be large, though not elected at large. Its size would serve to prevent political agency, but promote its role as a legislative body with the necessary staff to efficiently support that role. It would hold the executive agency accountable for programs, and be able to examine alternative ways of reaching educational objectives in addition to or instead of present school structures and systems. The Assembly would conduct audits of itself through outside sources, evaluate new programs with a specifically assigned internal agency, and would report to the public on a regular basis as to its findings, actions, or proposals. It would also sponsor the elections of governing boards for each agency and institution it authorizes. These local boards would act as community representatives for each agency or institution, and would hold the agency accountable and keep them close to the people served. The Assembly would work with other governmental agencies, unlike the present practice, and have the power to tax or borrow money, like the present practice. They would also promote the idea that schools are not the only place where learning can take place, and that children are not the school's only clients. Offshoots might include agencies for the arts, career education, guidance and evaluation, mini-schools, and adult centers.

Sarason employs a euphemism centered on the discussion of the place of boards of education by an optimist and pessimist, where the optimist says, "This is the best of all possible worlds," and the pessimist answers, "I'm afraid you are right." To the contrary, The Educational Assembly provides a means to concentrate political principle on a larger operating body that assigns agencies to concentrate on particular issues and study them in depth.

I advance that the Educational Assembly will work only when states fully understand the direction education needs to acquire. This must be fundamentally set at the national level, not by legislators, but by a coalition of industry officials, college faculty, and K-12 teachers. It must be specific enough so that all children in every state are healthy and cared for by exquisitely prepared teachers beginning in pre-K with small classes of no more than 15 children in grades K-3 particularly, and that expectations over broad age groups rather than grade levels are clearly defined. This accepts the proven reality that children, especially our youngest learners, grow at different rates. Testing should broadly determine where children are every few years, not every year, or twice a year. When deficiencies are discovered, methods based in research to help the child deal with a dysfunction should be put in place, and at the same, the strengths of the child, to include technology, the visual arts, and music, should be dynamically broadened. All this would include innovative activities that consume part of the summer vacation. Let's face it...it's too long and causes kids, especially kids with academic weaknesses, to lose ground. It also throws away the opportunity to create activities that are experiential and related to the work in the classroom. There are more innovations presented in later chapters. These are mentioned here to allow the reader to think what might be.

Community organizations like the Educational Assembly will work better in this environment. Here, their role is clearly defined and evaluated, not a happenstance of procedures, activities, and results that current boards of education represent. In terms of the award of tenure, they should have oversight as part of a group that reviews a teacher's accomplishments, but not the last word in its reward. That duty belongs to the superintendent, whose continued employment should be the assembly's responsibility. For its part, tenure is another institution that requires revision, as does the preparation of teachers.

Chapter 11
The Teacher—Preparation, Evaluation, and Tenure

James McBride, the noted jazz musician and author of the New York Times best-seller *The Color of Water,* stated to more than 2500 teachers at the July, 2004 National Advanced Placement Conference that:

Teachers are the last line of reason and discourse.

You are the curators of society.

Wow! I had never been so complemented—and I had never felt the weight of our responsibilities as much as I had when Mr. McBride put aside his saxophone and spoke those heartfelt words into his microphone (by the way, you ought to read James' book—it's incredibly touching and inspiring). It was a poetic call to duty, put into the most meaningful words I had ever heard directed to teachers. Every educator I spoke with in that room felt the same way. Indeed, others scribbled down those words as a new mantra.

My questions are: Are we up to being the last line of reason and discourse? What about the curators of society? I don't think so, and it's really not all our fault. However, we can act and direct efforts to change, or obviate our responsibilities and be changed. Resurrecting ineffective rote-based methods and educational procedures in the guise of NCLB mandates while we kept relatively silent unilaterally changed our classrooms and curricula.

I cannot think of anyone who gets into and stays in this business who has no passion for kids. It's too damned hard to stay if you don't. It's incredibly demanding, grinding, lonely work with little fanfare and few complements that is exacerbated by the present paradigms, and students who seem to come to us with more and more needs every year. Thus, teachers are working harder than ever.

Their creativity has been displaced by the need to get their children past tests, even those who have trouble getting to school.

While teaching is not recognized as a profession, it requires a graduate degree in order to maintain one's certification. Many who come to the classroom leave it after five years. As stated in my Foreword, the profession of teaching has been lock-stepped for over 100 years. Teachers have gained tremendous political clout, but the soul of what we do has been manipulated away from us. Tenure and pay have predominated the issues regarding the profession, rather than who is in charge of the teaching and learning process. While teachers either celebrated or castigated the provisions of NCLB, no great effort was made by powerful teacher organizations to lobby against it. After all, it was schools, school districts, and kids who would bear the brunt of it. Yet I wonder how far in the legislative process NCLB would have gotten if it had a provision to eliminate tenure.

On the other side of the coin, teachers are making considerably more money today than in years past. It is not uncommon to find a teacher salaried at $100,000+ on Long Island. While pay has increased, expectations of any real merit have not followed the rise in salaries. The school day remains at seven hours, and the school year still sits at 180 days. Nonetheless, teachers are increasingly frustrated, and though this frustration may have many sub-causes, the main cause is a system that stubbornly has not changed to incorporate the changes in society that make kids increasingly difficult to teach and guide in learning.

For example, what did schools do to change to accommodate the infusion of women into the workforce that began in earnest in the late 1970's? Women were expected to perform the jobs of mother and worker with the same aplomb. That men hadn't caught up to the times to assume a larger share of the keeping of the house and raising of the child made matters worse. When teachers called home, there was nobody there. Parent conferences were not as easy to schedule as they used to be. Did we accommodate this situation? Not at all. The workday still begins around 8:00 a.m. and still ends at 3:00 p.m., and the school year still begins around September 1 and ends around June 1. It's not that all parents don't care at all. They are just unable to care between 8:00 a.m. and 3:00 p.m. because they are out earning a living. "Latch-key" was a term we invented to describe children who went home to empty homes. We're good at inventing terms. We stink at inventing solutions that change education's structures and systems to accommodate the new circumstances children have to engage every day.

When I first began teaching in 1968, divorce afflicted one marriage in four. When I retired in 2004, the rate went to one in two.

We did little to accommodate the situation, except to note that when mothers entered the workforce or lost their husbands, the numbers of kids who wore the labels of special education increased, as did the failure rates. Nothing else changed. It made it easier to obviate our responsibilities with the blanket statement that parents didn't care. Yet we did nothing to allow them to care, or to demand that they care. We didn't change the model to allow real engagement of the child by providing parents the opportunity to be a part of it. Without new structures to provide opportunities for new engagement of the parent and child, and without a change in the vestigial 180-day/40-week school year and systems that lay the ground work for defining and treating dysfunction, demanding more of parents and kids or legislating laws that demand parental participation becomes a futile exercise. The sham of the ubiquitous "Open School Night" held once per year does not fill the bill—teachers lament that the parents who show up are the ones whose children are doing well. While there is a message here, it is better to avoid thinking about it as it might call the status quo into question, and, God forbid, we don't want to dally with that. Except to suffer the increasing numbers of failing or underachieving children, the teacher's job has not changed, yet the frustration level has grown commensurately with rising salaries. Those who enter the profession for the comparatively long vacation periods and early afternoon release need to reassess their priorities.

There is a body of research that suggests the variables of teacher salary and teacher performance do not correlate. Despite higher salaries, we have not had any dramatic increases in the numbers of students who choose to become teachers, nor has the quality of these students significantly risen to compete with those who may seek to become doctors, lawyers, or businessmen and businesswomen. Inner city teachers are still leaving the profession in droves before their third year. We have never been able to find enough math, science, or technology teachers. I offer that there are several issues at work here that need to addressed.

The career of teaching as it exists is just too demanding. Schools need to change dramatically to provide teachers a measure of success, to include smaller class sizes, smaller and better equipped buildings, and mandates placed on parents to provide support of their children in the school setting.

The school calendar and school day need to be adjusted to provide children and parents access to schools. I'm not so sure we need to be there the same five days a week each week or the same four weeks each month, or that we need five days per week each week. We definitely need to increase contact time between the school and the parent, and we're letting the summer go wanting.

There needs to be a regularly set time for teachers to talk deeply and reflectively about their practice and to openly discuss the work of their students, as research shows this type of staff development works best. One day a year with a powerhouse guest speaker or the consultant who does a reading workshop hasn't hurt, but it hasn't helped all that much.

Currently, teacher training does not equip the teacher-prospect with the skills needed for success. Teaching should not be the "lesser of the evil" majors that college students decide upon when they run out of options. Teacher training should:

Have student- teaching/classroom observations begin during the student's freshmen year, or sophomore year at the latest. The classroom, in all its known forms, and perhaps the forms that have yet to be invented, is where it's all at;

Require all teacher-candidates to be bilingual in Spanish. Face it—our population of Hispanics and Latinos grows each and every year. Denying it won't make our responsibilities go away or make for better engagement. We're doing English learners no good by shipping them off to ESL classes where everyone else is having the same problems learning English. Shipping children with special learning needs into homogeneous environments did not work either. Further, their parents should be learning English in mandated adult education programs as their children learn English (as the parents of special education students are learning about how they can aid in the education of their children);

Require that all teacher-candidates be certified in special education;

Require that secondary teachers be dually certified in two related areas (eg., math & science, English & second language, math & technology). Elementary level teachers need to be certified in a major discipline as well as elementary education and reading. Again, competency in a major discipline and reading requires less specialization where children are taken from their peers for remediation.

Require teacher candidates have multiple classroom experiences in multiple school districts;

Be six years in length to provide ample time to master all of the above tasks, to include the completion of courses towards the Master's Degree.

Be subsidized by the federal government at a flat rate of tuition. This subsidy should be increased when students show a particular propensity for success. College programs that produce successful teachers should be rewarded so they may award scholarships to attract the best prospects, as well as to conduct research studies that are based on excellent classroom practice.

Insure that the best teachers work in poverty-ridden school districts and the inner city schools by forgiving federal student loans and providing tuition rebates as a percentage of the undergraduate costs, and 100 percent of graduate level educational costs, should the teacher work at least ten years in the above stated environment.

In all of the above instances in regard to teacher preparation, or how student equity issues affect success, let this one axiom be known—dollars make scholars. Like I said in the Foreword, this is not going to be cheap to start, but in the ten-to-twenty-year long-term, significant savings in avoiding failure, "special placements," and promoting success will be garnered. In reflecting on this issue as I present it, please don't forget a few simple facts. A prison guard in New York State starts at $49,000 per year. It costs $60,000 to keep a kid in prison for one year. That $49,000 dollars is well earned by the guard I'm sure, but teachers' pay starts nowhere near that, and the teacher has a bachelor's degree. We shouldn't be surprised, as this is a signpost that we are an interventional, not a preventional, society. The cost for a bachelor's degree at a State University of New York (SUNY) campus is currently $60,000. Thus, when I propose that these better prepared, new Jedi-Knight teachers should start at least at $60,000, the cost seems more palatable, especially if we label more young people BA's, not JD's (juvenile delinquents), "perps," or repeat offenders. Teachers should reach their maximum pay after twenty years of service. Course credit for salary advancement should be given only for those courses taken at a college or a college-based institute that results in the reward of a second Master's degree, additional subject certification, or a doctorate. And graduate courses in the universities need to upgrade regularly to reflect emerging technologies, methodologies, and pedagogies. Master teachers, those with more than twenty years' service, should regularly teach them.

The issue of teacher tenure is hotly contested. It is rarely mentioned at all in reform literature, as it seems it is too hot a topic to discuss. Clearly, if we want to reform or eliminate other institutions as vestiges of days gone by, tenure as an institution needs to be addressed.

Tenure started out at the university level as a means to provide academic freedom. We didn't want any more of the treachery foisted on Galileo, who was forced upon threat of death to publicly negate his theories regarding the nature of the solar system that put the sun, not the earth, at its center, because it contradicted church dogma. Universities and colleges search for the truth with the research conducted by their faculties. Tenure guaranteed that the truth could be discussed as a frame of research without the threat of losing one's job. Tenure was adopted for similar reasons in the public schools to prevent vendettas from disgruntled parents or board of education members to make decisions as to what academic truth was. It was also a lure to keep teachers in the profession by practically providing life-long employment, as their wages were shamelessly low. It also protected those teachers who were long-time veterans from being fired for less expensive "rookie" teachers.

Now enter the $100,000 teacher, who with tenure is still promised lifetime employment, unless the teacher commits a felony. Poor performance in the classroom becomes a hard case to prove in removing a teacher's tenure, and it costs districts large sums of money they do not have. All know the system and how to beat it. Young teachers have learned to show their best efforts through the first three years of their employment, becoming involved in the school's extracurricular life, supportive of parents, and conducting superlative lessons. After the three-year probationary period, there is too often a slide in performance, though the majority of teachers keep developing and refining their practice. Yet, the best and those on their way to being the best and those who become the poorest are paid with the same guidelines – graduate courses taken and years of service. Performance in the classroom becomes a non-issue. This situation cannot stand, as the best teachers have little motivation to persist in the search for excellence while keeping their lower performing peers employed. In an age where individuals are downsized out of a job in flash and where employment hinges on performance, the situation in education is becoming more indefensible. If we are asking other institutions to reform or die off, teachers need to be guaranteed as the best to start, and to maintain that excellence through their careers.

Tenure has prohibited boards of educations with vendettas for some oddball reason or other to conduct a reign of terror, or politicians from exercising poor judgment based on emotion rather than research from conducting "house cleanings." Teaching is the only profession with such security, yet tenure is not awarded by peers, but by boards of education on the basis of recommendations from administrators. It is doctors and lawyers who decide who practices, and when malpractice occurs. Shouldn't teachers have a far greater voice in determining who is tenured and who is not? Wouldn't it be wise to extend the tenure period to five years, as it is in universities? Shouldn't tenure be reviewed after ten years of service, to take into account the totality of a teacher's performance to include success with students, community participation, professional contributions and memberships, and the continuity of involvement in pertinent graduate courses and staff development? If the teacher is found to be deficient, the reviewing board of teachers and administrators needs to put a comprehensive plan of staff development and mentoring into place to improve the teacher's performance, and the teacher must show evidence of implementing that plan by measured improvement.

I mentioned that teacher retirement should be mandated after twenty years. That is, teachers should be invited to stay after this point, or should decide themselves that their lives need to take a different direction. Those who are asked to stay should be able to leave the classroom for periods of time and pursue interest in administration, counseling, or research. Better yet, because they have been recognized as the best, they should be mentoring and evaluating new staff, teaching at colleges, developing training for other staff members, and visiting other schools with programs recognized as superlative, in addition to maintaining their classroom practice. They should be key in designing new structures and systems. They also should be highly compensated so their interest in the classroom remains steadfast, and they do not have to enter the ranks of administration to make more money as many of the best teachers do. After all, if they are universally recognized as the last line of reason and discourse and the curators of society, and that mission is best practiced and refined in the laboratory of the classroom in all its present and future guises.

Are there models out there for teacher preparation programs to emulate? Jaime Escalante had a movie made about his efforts in a Los Angeles school called *Stand and Deliver*. I would strongly suggest that the readers of this text read *Freedom Writers* by Erin Gruhill. Erin, a delightful young woman, transformed an inner-city school in Long Beach in her first year as a teacher. Chauncy Veatch, a retired army colonel, taught Chicano kids to learn and to maintain hope in a small Southern California border town. His efforts had him recognized as the National Teacher of the Year in 2002. Listening and talking to each of them is inspirational. Both worked magic with their passion, persistence, a love of their kids, and as an absolute hatred for failure. Each of them rewrote the rules as they went. I would venture that as they would read this chapter, they would bubble over with new ideas, some complementary, some oppositional. Nonetheless, their new ideas would be born of solid practice in the classroom.

Chapter 12
Disconnects Between Goals, Practice, and the National Good

Our number one product as a nation is Intellectual Capital. It has surpassed our production of hard goods and soft goods. We are now selling our brainpower, not as a creator of a product, but as a product itself, clear and simple. It is a clear link to what I introduced as edu-prise in Chapter 4. We do it better than anyone else in the world. I think one of the reasons that this is so is that we encourage intentionality, the human desire to create, to experiment, and to challenge the unknown. The problem is, we don't encourage this in the K-12 schools not nearly as much as we should, and if we did, we can sell a whole lot more brainpower. Instead, we make up rules to force compromise and conformity, to accompany the conformity now demanded by standards-based curriculum and its accompanying high stakes tests. Some of them are just inhumane.

Twist it and turn it as you might, compliance is a matter of students being forced to do things they don't want to do. They rebel outwardly or as Ghandi-esque passive resistors. Either way, if they refuse to learn, they are not going to learn. They are not stupid, and they realize it when a rule is made to make some adult feel better rather than to insure their protection and safety to precipitate better learning. Forcing compliance forces non-compliance, and while kids are rebelling and teachers and administrators are chasing them down, learning is the last thing taking place. Enforcement of the rules supersedes the purpose of the schools. While learning needs to be disciplined, discipline in schools is not about learning. With the advent of site-based management teams, socially and economically empowered parents are trying to recreate the school within their own narrow image, while those parents who are not socially empowered and economically disenfranchised have to abide by the rules wrought in an attempt to make every kid the same cookie-cutter image. It's culture against culture. Learning, again, plays second fiddle.

As a senior in high school, I remember back in 1963 when the Beatles appeared on The Ed Sullivan Show and took the nation by storm. A few months later, boys' hair became a bit longer, because girls were taken with the hairstyles of the Beatles. A big furor in schools took place when hair got longer, that the end of our way of life was one missed haircut away. With the advent of the miniskirt, girls' knees became more conspicuous, a sure indication that our morals were going to hell. Long hair and short skirts needed to be attacked by schools as anti-American culture. Yet, kids learned and we survived. When hair got short, or dreadlocks became the style, many suspected something was up, and whatever it was, it wasn't good. Beards became prominent, and so again did rumors of our imminent collapse. Yet, kids learned and we survived. When kids wore piercings or dyed their hair weird colors, rumors abounded that the apocalypse was just around the corner—again. Yet, we survived (though I really worry about the scars piercing leaves—but, it's not my skin!). Then, the final slap in the face to polite society – hats!—hats, worn backwards, or upside down, or with their brims off to one side; hats, the icon of evil and ne'er-do-wells! Funny thing, but there aren't any studies out there that say SAT scores go down when kids wear, or don't wear, hats.

Do you get the idea that the things we spend a good deal of time in discussing, and the salary of assistant principals in rule-enforcing, don't matter a tinker's damn in determining what kids learn, or what we teach? Things like Vietnam, Watergate, Iran-Gate, the Deficit, Civil Rights, Medicare, Social Security, Enron, and now the Iraqi occupation are not seen to be as important in determining where society was heading as what kids were doing with their hair, beards, skirts, piercings, and hats. In this context, it is also deemed more important for kids to ask permission to empty their bodies of waste, to take care of sanitary concerns, or to simply wash their hands because if they did these normally human things without permission, surely the Communists would take over. When we ran out of Communists, we figured the Germans or Japanese would rise up again to end our way of life because they were selling more cars here than GM, Ford, or Chrysler, and kids not asking permission to go to the bathroom would hasten our deaths at their evil, manipulating hands. Some may say that dress codes and bathroom passes are a way of maintaining discipline. I say they are poor excuses used to keep up the facade that schools are effective based on the depth of their "will nots." What is learned, how it is learned, and how many kids are engaged in learning becomes second tier stuff. Bathroom passes and kids walking around bareheaded are deemed true signs of effectiveness. What is lacking in all this is the fact that not one college in evaluating students for admission asks about the school's bathroom pass policy, or the policy on headgear- it is test scores, teacher performance, and administrative effectiveness that are measured in the context of the effectiveness of the classroom. In short, what are you teaching, are your programs growing in scope and sequence, and are kids learning- these are the questions whose answers come out in the data that colleges look at to admit or deny kids. If kids aren't willingly in the classroom, something is not happening in that classroom that should be happening. A hat or a nose ring is not a clear indicator of this, and if kids would rather be in the bathroom than in the classroom...well, I'll let the reader decide the thought processes that bring them to that conclusion.

Based on the points offered in the chapters prior to this, schools should be run on the premise that learning takes place every minute of every hour of every day, and kids hold major responsibility for that process. If schools are structured this way, and if a student still is not participative in the process, the student needs to assume an academic price, and the co-payees should include the parents. As mentioned, the word "parent" is not only a noun, but also a verb that denotes an action process. If schools are smaller, well-funded, experientially directed, well led with the inclusion of student voice, and equipped with first-rate teachers as described herein, kids and parents should assume more of the outcome of their own educational fate. If parents do not come to the school, teachers should have time to go to the parents—at home or at their place of work, to voice their concerns about their child's learning, not their bathroom habits. If students fail, they need to do it over, but we should not tolerate "do-overs" as an automatic endowment of a free public education. We have other things on which to spend money than a family of recalcitrants who obviate their responsibilities by not demanding that their children attend school or be engaged. Somewhere in all this, a monetary fine, however small, needs to be exacted. We simply cannot allow those non-educated to be a drain on the rest of us, if it is determined that the cause of their non-education has nothing to do with the student's ability or inability to learn. Really good, restructured schools, ably led with sound curricular and positive child-centered practices with solid parental support, can demand the best that kids have to offer.

That said, schools need to adjust their schedules to provide time for students who struggle. This would include the offerings of summer semesters that are preventional, in that kids with academic difficulties who attend and are academically frustrated, are engaged prior to their failure. Kids who want to get ahead can use the summer to bolster their skills or complete courses to make more time available in the fall or spring for other courses they would want to take. As I mentioned before, the idea that kids who are not specifically four-year college-bound should take as much math and science as those who are, rather than courses that illuminate their talents rather than their weaknesses, is preposterous, but that is what some states consider "raising the bar." I would love to apply this same thinking to have kids who are "art-less" or "technology-less" forced to suffer through graphic arts, painting and drawing, cabinet-making, video production, or cosmetology. Many would consider this cruel and unusual punishment. If at all, math and science needs to be taught in the context of these technological courses, not as it is taught to those seeking a traditional four-year college experience. Recall as well that only fifty-three percent of those who start college finish. Perhaps "raising the bar" needs to be defined in a new context. It certainly won't be raised by ridiculous non-sequitur pedagogical demands, or silly rules made to help a few paranoid and fearful adults gain a degree of false comfort.

The community colleges need to be further recognized as key to America's educational resurgence. They currently provide a grand second chance to kids who, one way or the other, were disaffected by high school, to those who "catch fire" later on, to who don't have enough money to go to a four-year college immediately after high school, as well as to adults who need to be retrained in occupations that are dependent on emerging technologies. I see the concept of edu-prise relying on a hard and fast relationship with business and industry for these emerging technologies to be recognized and packaged for the purposes of rapid retraining of a population who is well prepared by the K-12 system to listen, think, and learn. No one should be denied the chance to start over, become better, or learn something different. This is a democratic ideal.

Edu-prise depends on a lifetime of educational access. More importantly, it depends on students who have been educated to realize that the educational process is an affirmative experience that magnifies their strengths while accommodating their weaknesses. It also depends on continuous support and participation by business and industry to keep what is needed to be known as timely and readily distributed to a constantly renewed and redefined knowledge base.

When one is truly educated, the individual becomes more involved with his or her being, and the being of others. The world becomes clearer; the educated become acutely aware that they have to examine differences and similarities beyond the surface. With this, not only do their brains work better—so do their hearts.

Chapter 13
"My Grandmother Wants to Fly Jets!"
(Or, What It Takes To Lead)

Remember the movie *An Officer and a Gentleman*? Louis Gosset Jr. won an Oscar for his portrayal of a tough Marine drill sergeant whose mission was to drum out individuals from the ranks of those who thought they had the right stuff to be air officer candidates, the Navy's future Top Guns. You will also recall that Richard Gere played an officer candidate whose character was not in line with what the Navy expected of its pilots. In a scene that had Gosset's character literally torturing Gere's character with the hope that he would drop out of the program, Gosset asks him why he wants to continue the abuse he is enduring. Through the pain, Gere blurts out, "I want to fly jets!" Gosset's character retorts, "My grandmother wants to fly jets!"

Why do I use this metaphor? Simply to explain that those who wish to lead schools as administrators have to display more than a desire to satisfy an ego or make more money. If teachers are to be the last resort of discourse and reason and the curators of society, it would follow that those who choose to lead them should really be something extra special. Either by systemic design or error in appointment procedures or evaluations, this is not always the case.

A close friend worked in a district with two middle schools literally the mirror image of each other, separated from each other by a few miles of Interstate. He worked as a teacher in one, and interned for his administrative certification in the other. He immediately noted the differences. In one school, teachers complained bitterly about everything and anything. The kids weren't up to the task of learning, they said. There were no evening dances or events, other than athletic contests. There wasn't much innovation in the classroom. Problem students dominated the school's operation. In the school in which he interned, teachers roared in every day. They laughed and joked and socialized with each other. Kids were motivated and spent a good deal of time with their teachers after school. There were problem students to be sure, but they were not allowed to dominate the educational landscape. Teachers made full use of the technology that was available.

The event he said that magnified the difference between the schools was a holiday concert, held in both schools on the same night. The principal of the school in which my friend interned asked him to stop by so he could introduce him formally to the parents. He could then proceed to his own school's concert. He pulled into the driveway of his intern building, and froze—the lot was packed with cars. He thought that perhaps he got the time wrong. He parked and ran breathlessly into the building, and found the principal amiably talking to parents in the foyer. It wasn't that he was late—parents had come early to get seats. The auditorium was packed, each of its three aisles filled with parents. A Minorah outlined in holiday lights decorated one wall. The other wall was decorated with lights outlining a Christmas tree. The curtain opened, and students were gathered around a fireplace, singing familiar holiday tunes, and began their concert with a comical skit about one of their teachers.

Time was short. He hurried the few miles to his own building and pulled into the lot. There were hardly any cars to be found. Did he have the right date? He heard music that wasn't very festive coming from the auditorium. He entered to find the room barely a third full. There were no decorations. The curtain on the stage hung off its tracks.

Two identical middle schools in the same district, the same kinds of kids—what made the difference? I would think it was one of expectations and the philosophy of the principals involved.

Leaders set the tone. They are the source of energy. They sweat the details. They inspire and evaluate staff, motivate them, and set expectations. They provide and interpret policy. They execute the policy of the school district, but are obviously allowed enough space to implant their own methodologies and practices to carry it out. They lead through hard work, example, and high expectations. They stay informed and current on educational issues. They are one step ahead.

Some administrators see discipline as a role onto itself, rather than imbued by the rigor and excitement of a dynamic academic and extracurricular program delivered by teachers who know what is expected of them. Teachers are regularly evaluated formally and informally. While much is demanded, they require much support.

Students know the expectations of them as well, as their teachers practice rigorously and show them respect. While teaching different subjects in different ways, teachers insure that students know they are the focal point of instruction. Clearly, administrators need to be part and parcel of this process, not lurking on the fringes with the threat of punishment for teachers and students as their only purpose.

How are administrators appointed? Most states have certification requirements that require a graduate degree in school administration for teachers to be certified as chairpersons, assistant principals, principals, assistant superintendents, and superintendents. After this requirement, the choice of administrators takes on a number of variations on the theme.

Many times, administrators are chosen from the teachers' ranks because they were excellent disciplinarians, and discipline is a main concern, especially in the secondary schools. Good discipline is synonymously assumed to be a requisite of solid instructional practices. Others, those I feel are the most successful, are chosen because they are recognized by the depth and breadth of their teaching, where discipline evolves from the positive engagement of youngsters, not as an entity onto itself. Others have a track record of achieved leadership and can get things done or can build consensus. Some are appointed by virtue of their sex, others by political will. Some are cheaper to hire than others, especially if they are moving from a poorly paid city position to a more lucrative suburban district. Still others are chosen because they excel in golf or strike an impressive image, or make it known they are actively seeking a particular administrative title. Still others feel endowed.

An advanced degree beyond certification is not often deemed important. Leadership or active participation in a professional organization at the local, regional, or national level is overlooked. Innovative incidents of practice in the classroom do not seem to hold much water either. As stated, those who are strict classroom disciplinarians usually get the nod, as it is assumed that discipline in a singular classroom can be compounded across an entire school. A breadth of experiences in a few school districts, or a major role in an innovative program is often overlooked. Some districts decide it is safer to hire from within, as they have a well-known track record to review, and while they may seek change, the person they are considering to appoint is a known entity, one who promises that things will be different, though they often do not know what "different" is. The fear factor gets a good deal of play in choosing administrators. Teaching as an art does not, nor does innovative practice or a wide breadth of experiences.

As I mentioned before, discipline should not become an instructional end in its own right. It is a function of dynamic classrooms and school buildings. Assistant principals and deans of students (among other titles) are assigned the maintenance of discipline—too many times, you have to be able to have demonstrated that you gave kids detention or suspended them to be considered for higher administrative positions. Who is assigned the maintenance of rigorous, dynamic instruction? It appears that no one is, unless schools have subject-specific chair people who are empowered to observe teachers, create instances of meaningful staff development, and write curriculum, but the discipline factor usually excludes them from higher level administrative jobs. Teachers appreciate the practice of hiring from within just as board of education members do—they know what they are getting. If discipline is the main concern and candidates are hired from within, teachers come to understand that their disciplinary methods are validated. They do not have to change the instructional methods bred from the culture with which they engage kids. The status quo remains unperturbed.

Administrators rarely come from areas outside the traditional classroom as it is thought that they can have very little empathy for the work that occurs in that basic building block of instructional delivery. Counselors, special education teachers, and physical education teachers may have a difficult time understanding the dynamic of the traditional classroom. This, however, can be a blessing in disguise if the administrator is willing to dialogue and think because the methodologies they used in their unique subject areas may lead to innovation, as these particular curricular disciplines are very much children-centered. Still, the question of leadership and participation in the dialogue of education as provided by external organizations remains an important factor.

The prospect of tenure rears up again with administrators. Having achieved tenure in a school district, the administrator-in-waiting considers the risk of losing tenure to assume another administrative position as unacceptable. There is very little reason to venture beyond well-known borders if the parameters of the award of tenure, to include expectations and evaluations, are familiar operations. It seems, then, that hiring from within weakens the breed, as those who venture out of tenure's familiar comfort zone to entirely different districts to learn a different culture or a variety of educational ways and means, are the real risk-takers in learning about change.

Innovation is a fleetingly temporal practice. What is new today is old tomorrow. Administrators are sometimes hired to establish a well-known or innovative program in a school district. Five years later, after data indicate that the innovation has become stale or anachronistic in practice, the program continues to soak up funds and staff. Yet, the administrator clings to this one bright and shining moment well into his or her career.

Administrators need to come to grips with the fact that it was solely their choice that empowered them to the level of the educational hierarchy they seek. Those who they lead are just as bright, innovative, and concerned with kids as they are—maybe more so. They just chose to remain in the classroom, as it is here that they derive their greatest satisfaction. In the professional context, teaching is everything and the only thing to them. To ask administrators how, what, and why they think as they do is considered a dangerous exercise for many of them, as they feel the administrator will take any comment as a challenge to newly acquired power. What some administrators fail to realize is that power comes in two forms—ascribed power and achieved power. Ascribed power is that which comes with the definition of the job. To evaluate teachers, check their lesson plans, and to discipline students are examples of ascribed power. Achieved power is derived from those who are led. Faith in the leadership's ability to communicate and to build consensus on important issues is achieved power. In essence, it is the better of the two powers to have. It is kinetic and in constant use. It is re-energized daily. It allows for voice and growth. It is hard to do because it takes an enormous amount of faith in one's abilities and trusting those to be led. However, it produces the best results. Ascribed power speaks of potential, of what might be if it is exercised judiciously in the quest for achieved power. Potential power is nice to talk about—kinetic power gets things done, and done much better because a group of fine minds socially constructed its use and feel comfortable in operationalizing its outcomes.

Narrow administrative martinets usually wind up stifling innovation and voice. They feel most comfortable on image-building exercises, such as insisting on dress codes for teachers or no hats for kids, rather than the stuff of real instructional innovation. They know all the answers, and in their myopic assumptions, they set up systems based on the narrowness of their own experiences as to what works best. They have their teacher favorites that they imbue with all sorts of privilege, even if these favorites are causing academic doldrums and stagnant practice to the disdain of their teacher peers. Dialogue is discouraged systemically. Intimidation, the use of which is especially a sign of the weakest, wears out quickly as a methodology of management. Depth and breadth provide a richer depository of innovative capability.

Think of this—administrators hire and recommend tenure for teachers. If the teachers are encultured with such negativity, or if teachers are given tenure based solely on their ability to keep good discipline, the problem of poor administrators becomes multiplied geometrically.

The traditional administrative flow chart of job titles and responsibility needs to be reviewed. For example, as previously mentioned, even if No Child Left Behind promotes degenerative methods and instructional models that rely on tests of questionable content and purpose, it did give us lots of data to review. How many districts created the title of Chief Information Officer to investigate the data in terms of test correlations between state tests and national tests, correlations and differences among teachers, how grade level curricular responsibilities leading up to a test are met, or how kids from different schools compare and differ? The individual charged with this function can produce glaring data that may show how badly a district or school missed its NCLB mark, or struck a bull's eye. More than this, information can be presented to teachers in meaningful ways. Were various math and reading programs investigated with an in-depth analysis of testing data? Are testing practices and teacher practices correlated from marking period to mid-term to final exam? How do they differ? Do they incorporate the engagement of national exams? In one school district with which I was familiar, mid-term exams were put into effect with the assumed wild-eyed premise that they would help with SAT scores, as students were thought not to have enough experience taking three-hour exams. No mind was given to the fact that the SAT is an aptitude test charged with predicting college success, and that teacher-created exams and final exams were achievement tests based on a preset curriculum. Twenty years later, the SAT scores never improved and failures increased, but mid-terms were kept as practice because the exams were assumed to keep teachers up to date with curriculum delivery. As a result, kids were still taking incredibly punitive three-hour long exams solely to keep their teachers on task. Teachers were not held accountable. There never was a stitch of research done to prove the effectiveness of the exams in helping kids learn either prior to or after the institution of the midterm policy. No correlational studies with the SAT, marking period grades, state exams, or final exams were ever undertaken. Again, a "get tough" policy was used to disguise the fact that deep thinking about academic performance improvement was too difficult a task to undertake, or beyond the capacity of those in charge to improve. A ludicrous practice continued.

Do we still need the traditional administrative titles? How does an assistant principal actually assist the principal? If the assistant principalship is preparation for the principalship, what other measures besides disciplinary actions or managerial efficiency are used to determine the capacity of the assistant principal for leadership of an entire school? Does the job title automatically denote the job practice? What does a deputy superintendent do that an assistant superintendent does not? What do directors actually direct? How close are all of these to the practice of the classroom? Are roles reviewed and modified with the times? Do administrators use data as a shield, or as an impetus for deep inquiry? What about the broad coordination of ancillary services? With the growth of special education, is it really still special? With so many specialists working with so many kids, how can this be effectively monitored on a daily basis? Is it part of the reason that so many kids get into special education, but never get out?

There is an old saying that if administrators don't feed the teachers, the teachers will eat the kids. Generally, administrators who are crack disciplinarians or those without a variety of experiences see the world myopically. They stand on ceremony, tired old traditions, and try to save the world entirely on their own in their narrow view of it. The forest is lost for the trees. Teachers lose faith. The kids soon follow. The parents sense it almost immediately from the tenor of the school. What's going on is as plain as the decorations, or lack of them, on the auditorium walls.

There is an interesting management philosophy outlined in the book *Good to Great* by Jim Collins that spends a good deal of print on the methodology of placing the right people in the right job with the right job title. It should serve as required reading for administrators and administrators-to-be, right there on the bookshelf next to Peter Senge's work.

Chapter 14
The School Counselor—Messenger, Architect, and Confidant

If teachers are to assume new roles and refined practices to validate their responsibilities as the last line of reason and discourse and the curators of society, certainly counselors should be included within this definition. Counseling in itself is based on reason and discourse, and counseling as a device should monitor societal changes that directly effect the world of children. For this to really happen, counselor training and practice needs to change.

Counselors are the school's eyes and ears in the community. They should scan the workforce for changes by integrating their efforts with state and federal officials who are responsible for monitoring the economy. Through the college admissions process, they constantly come to understand how education beyond the high school is changing, and keep their fellow educators informed so they can determine the appropriate steps to keep curricula up to date. They are the conduits of the affective realm of education. Too many times, they represent the last resort for troubled kids whose families have turned on them, who the school has put out on the fringes, or that society has shut out. They see the child as the child first, and a student second. They are equipped with the skills to listen, and listen again. There is no judgment such as a grade that hangs in the balance when kids and counselors talk. What results, hopefully, is a better vision of reality, and how the child can take part in the world rather than being marginalized from it.

The school calendar and its daily schedule may artificially put limits on the process of formal education, but in this context as presented, the child lives, and life around the world goes on. Families still need information or help, as do children when July comes. The school prepares for the coming September during the summer. The world doesn't go on "spring break." People are doing the chores of life at night and on weekends, and believe it or not, during the summer, mid-winter, and the spring. If anyone needs flexibility to meet the needs of the population, it is the counselor.

This has presented a two-pronged problem—counselors normally do not want to work when their classroom-based colleagues may be on vacation. Secondly, despite the fact that life goes on when classroom instruction ceases, districts have assumed for their own benefit that the counselor's role is the same the teacher's role, and do not want to have counselors working when teachers are not. In the academic context, this causes a number of missteps, especially as it pertains to the summer as the time for remediation (and perhaps one day the time for enrichment and advancement) and preparation for the coming year. At the secondary level, students need to have their academic programs reset to compensate for failure, success, or a change of mind. The only person who keeps track of all this and advises the student as to the options their school provides is the counselor. They are the globalists in a world of subject area specialists and administrative managers. When this is not done in July or August, chaos reigns supreme in September. Fully three or four weeks of instruction go wanting as students try to change an errant program of classes. At the elementary level, work that was done to help socialize a child or provide direction for families in crisis goes lacking over the summer. As systemically inefficient as the school is, this is one of the flavors of icing on the cake that contributes to its ineffectiveness.

Some schools try to compensate for this "slack time" by having counselors work in a compensatory arrangement, meaning that they are allowed to take time off during the school year that is commensurate to the time they worked during the summer. What this means is that counselors become unavailable to do their jobs when the students are the most readily accessible. If counselors are clerks and not accepted as highly trained and skilled professionals as described in the first paragraph of this chapter, this would make sense. However, if service to the child and community are the primary purposes of counselors, compensatory time is absurd.

Counselors need to do some of their work in the evenings and during the traditional but vestigial vacation periods. Yet, they need to be there for kids and teachers to make the necessary links to the home and to the community when the calendar and school day says they can. A child cannot plan a crisis around the counselor's schedule, nor a family, nor a school for that matter. Would counselors have taken compensatory time on September 12, 2001 and the immediate few days thereafter? The summer is an important academic time, though the vestigial calendar and the accompanying budgeting arrangements at the state and local levels would have us think that the world stops in June and picks up again in September, and we can throw away two precious months while the kids stay home "to work the family farms." Perhaps this might be a factor in the farming and ranching states, but aside from these particular regions, the calendar makes little sense.

Counselors, therefore, need realistic caseloads, flexible schedules, and higher compensation to work a longer day and longer school year. Unlike teachers, they do not have to be in classes every day, but do need to be there more often than not. They also need to run programs in the evening and on weekends for parents who cannot make it during the normal school day, school week, or school year, so as to expand the community's horizons and its understanding of its schools. They cannot be responsible for more than 200 students at the high school level, and no more than 300 at the middle school level at the maximum. Elementary level caseloads need to be decided by the activities of the counselor at this level. The rare breed known as the elementary school counselor needs to be better defined in the context of the counselor's work as described above. They cannot be pseudo-assistant principals or behaviorists, nor should they be seen as therapists, or the arm of teachers who see their main function as instruction and not at all concerned with the child's affective domain.

To do this, counselor training programs need to be redefined. More research-based courses need to be implemented, as counselors should have a notion of how to study trends, programs, test results, and community-generated data. They need to be able to interpret data provided by various organizations and the district's chief information officer to make it more meaningful as to what is happening with kids. They need to be experts on how the various curriculum strands come together to the benefit or handicap of a child. In summary, they should be globalists who see the totality of the school's effect on the student, to include the work of psychologists, social workers, and learning specialists. Through these actions, they need to inform curriculum. Metaphorically, their distance from the classroom should be measured in feet, not yards. To this end, they should not at all be strangers to instruction and instructional methodologies and strategies.

School counselors are not therapists, but school counselor preparation programs largely ignore research-based activities in favor of courses regarding deep study in therapeutic theory and practice which most counselors rarely have the opportunity to do. Psychologists may have the opportunity to practice in this direction, but can also administer psychometric measures to provide additional direction in diagnosing and defining a child's dysfunction.

Counselor time can be better spent in delivering guidance services in the classroom, to include information pertinent to all students. This is not to say they should abandon their individual and group counseling sessions with students. However, there is much to transmit and the best place to do this is in the classroom, the center of reform, relating up-to-date information concerning the student's immediate and long-term future. In short, the counselor needs to be an articulate messenger of things to come and an architect of how the student can best be academically positioned to take full advantage of arising opportunities.

When the counselor does play the messenger, in this case to administrators, role confusion is sometimes an outcome. A fellow guidance director related a story about her superintendent going a bit bonkers because the district's SAT scores did not improve. He took his venom out on her, a counselor. The superintendent obviously does not realize it, but for the sake of informing him and others like him, the counselors do not teach math or English. They do not prepare their students directly for the SAT, save to do a few class visits to let kids know when the tests are, how to register for them, and perhaps distribute some test-taking hints The College Board offers for distribution, and to include information about The Board's website. Perhaps the counselor is even in charge of the high school when it becomes a test center for the SAT. That's about it. The SAT tests verbal and mathematical skills, and beginning in March of 2005, it will also test writing adeptness. The last time I checked, these test categories fell into the realm of the math and English teachers. Blaming the counselors for the lack of scholarships students receive or their denial at the most selective colleges is like killing the messenger. Scholarships and college admission are based in part on achievement as well as on SAT scores, and SAT scores depend on instruction in mathematics and English, as well as an informed and academically aggressive population.

Superintendents' lack of insight into role identification is strikingly disturbing. The SAT and the college admissions process is not a public relations problem, nor are they a "quick fix" item. They point to the health of the school system, from classroom instruction to communication with parents and faculty. Along with the SAT, a high school's AP participation, from the numbers of courses offered to the numbers of students who take an AP exam, tell a story of confidence and competitiveness that takes its root in a sound curricular structure. Kids need to feel confident about their chances, and faculty members need to build a confidence level, too. This is done by staff development, something the makers of the SAT and AP exams and The College Board stress. Counselors are intimately involved in telling students and parents about the importance of AP courses and SAT and AP exams, and in using them to help frame a student's future possibilities by interpreting exam results. Holding counselors accountable for the outcomes of standardized testing shows a disturbing lack of breadth and leadership.

I remember spending hours gathering data for an SAT improvement study for which one of our assistant superintendents had been assigned by the superintendent. We met to examine the data and discovered some interesting trends. Directors of English and Math pored over the data, made a few suggestions, and everyone shook their heads in agreement as to what the data said. The meeting ended without any solution as to how scores would improve, how teachers would be trained, or how curriculum goals would change to incorporate the SAT. Examining the data was obviously the implied improvement plan. Nothing else happened, despite my repeated reminders that academic processes and curricula needed to change for students to more successfully engage this exam. The SAT scores never improved (the whole of student achievement never did), yet I was asked time and again why more kids weren't getting scholarships or getting accepted to more selective colleges, the questioners now including board of education members. Strangely, those charged with math and English never answered the questions, but then again, they were never asked. More than the exception, this experience is the rule for counselors.

As stated, counselors are not administrators. They are not there to help with "administrivia" to the point where they are not seeing kids, interpreting trends, or reaching out to the community. They are not there to waste time on public relations gimmicks that school districts are taken with to make the district look good when they have no real meaning for kids. For example, counselors spend hours poring over class lists of students' academic averages and SAT scores that are used to qualify for the dubious President's Academic Fitness Awards. This nonsense goes back to the Reagan era, where a non-descript lapel pin and a certificate "signed" by the president himself is given to high school seniors, sort of like a presidential "attaboy" for solid academic achievement. While elementary school children might "ooh and aah" at this gift from their president, seniors need money for college, not a worthless certificate and a pin a kid wouldn't be caught dead wearing. It's bad enough that counselor time is being preyed upon by the endless, and often contradictory, record-keeping required by states and the federal NCLB, working with student management computer systems that have not caught up to the requirements, and propping up a system bent on destroying academic rigor and content.

Their time shouldn't be preyed upon with nebulous trivia that looks good on public relations paper, but does little to enhance a student's possibilities. A Presidential Academic Fitness Award has as much clout on college admissions applications or a résumé as a piece of Charmin. It misleads the public and the kids into thinking that something grander is happening behind that glitzy piece of paper and that fancy pin.

If districts are desperate enough to need this kind of positive spin, they should let someone else, besides a highly trained and expensive counselor, do the screening of grades and SAT scores. It should also prompt the government to realize that the paper generated by NCLB is quite enough in itself to keep all educators busy. It should be reminded as well that college tuition and fees for many of those Fitness Awards winners is out of reach, in large part due to misguided fiscal policies. For example, rather than conjuring up another pointless public relations program or another innocuous unfunded mandate, the government might better concentrate on the Pell Grant Program, which has not increased in real dollars since its 1974 inception. Then counselors can do real work in getting more kids transitioned to college.

Chapter 15
Boarding the Starship Edu-Prise—
The Bottom Line

Forgive my "Trekiness", but herewith are recommendations complementing those previously stated to begin the end of educational gridlock and lunacy. Each one of the items previously recommended or contained below could serve as the topic for a book or doctoral study in its own right. I still maintain we will save much more in a generation than we are spending in a failing effort now. Do-overs and perpetrating the present hoax costs us much more, in both monetary and human terms. We owe kids a better shot at education than they are getting now. We also owe it to ourselves.

Remember I defined edu-prise in Chapter 4 as an aggressive pursuit of educational reform that puts purpose into the system, rather than continues with repetitive exercises that continually frustrate and fail to one degree or another all who come in contact with it. I just completed reading *The Two Percent Solution* by Matthew Miller, who addresses the shortcomings of education and gives his own ideas as to how it could change. We agree on some of this, but I expand Miller's recommendations to include systemic overhaul of the whole of education, not just the work of the teacher. I mention it here because Miller offers that the failing public systems that plague us, to include education, can be fixed by a slight increase in spending. Miller warns that we need to act NOW, not ten years from now when the system will be bankrupt when the "Baby Boomers" retire. I concur fully, and not only from an economic point of view—we are compromising young lives, if not outwardly, then in failing to do something more to save them. We need to make things a whole lot better if we are to attract the best and brightest to our classrooms to save them. Please keep this in mind as you review the listing below:

We cannot rely solely on property taxes to fund schools. We cannot sustain the lunacy of politics as usual to avoid doing the right thing to make schools equitable. This issue needs to be solved at the state and federal level. It would be cheaper for all of us if the primary funding for schools came from a more centralized location. If schools wanted to add enhancements, property taxes could supplement federal and state grants to schools, much as is done now. However, there needs to be a review state-by-state, county-by-county, school district-by-school district to determine funding formulae so schools in poor areas can offer comparable services compared to their wealthier counterparts.

Large schools, especially those over fifty years old, need heavy modification to make them smaller, more responsive, and more people-friendly than the dinosaurs we have. We simply cannot allow schools to be impersonal to kids as much as society tends to be. Every kid needs to know that he or she is valued. Parents need to know we care. In fact, we should demand that they care, and do it legislatively. We've come up with dumber unenforceable laws that do not work, like not using a cell phone when driving. Look over at the person in the next lane of the expressway to see how well that one is working. Perhaps if an accident occurs, and the cell phone record indicates it was in use at that exact time, the driver needs to be more heavily penalized than a fine. It is sort of like our approach to education. We know we are not doing the right thing by passing standards-based laws that assume every kids is equal in intellect, interest, and aptitude. When we finally admit they are not, it is usually too late, and the cost for the do-over is much more extraordinary, to say nothing of what it will cost to repair a kid's self-image.

Why do we need school five days per week every week? Why don't we lengthen the day and the school year a bit, and have school four days per week so we can develop staff and meet with parents on a consistent basis? We also need to come up with creative uses of the summer, and not just waste it on remediation. Two or three intense summer sessions would do much to help kids catch up, get ahead, display an interest, study something they cannot study during the school year, or provide general access to learning. Ten weeks is a long time without instruction or academic stimulation.

Testing requirements need to be made more fluid where tests are such a big part of the educational landscape. If we are married to the damned things for the time being, we should allow kids more opportunities to pass them. When we come up with true National Standards born out by colleges and industries, not legislators and state education departments which have generally lost touch with reality in their zeal to make our system "world class" and qualify for federal dollars under NCLB, we need to re-work testing in scope and sequence. Education cannot be yesterday's exercise as the present system forces it to be, but one born of tomorrow that constantly changes to meet changing needs.

As a corollary, all secondary school kids should not be required to pass the same tests. We need to differentiate what we require based on what kids have told us they would like to pursue, and the standards they measure should be based on what colleges and industries tell us is important.

Elementary level tests should be purely diagnostic, and their results reviewed with all stakeholders, to include the parent and child. Some tests need to be given more often than at particular grade levels to determine how children are progressing. If schools are set up as I suggested (smaller schools with smaller classes, year-round calendars, well-fed kids, excellent teachers, parent-mandated participation) the reasons for failure might now point to real disabilities and the creation of better pedagogical paradigms to remediate them.

Strengthen the community colleges. They are most important in re-doing education. They need a national mission and money to succeed in insuring we all have an opportunity to redirect our lives, strengthen our skills, or provide cutting edge technological training. There are studies that show students who graduate from community colleges and attend four-year colleges afterwards still require remediation. This cannot continue.

Ungrade grades K, one, and two. They worked better years ago in the little red schoolhouse. Rather than relying solely on grade level curricula, use this time period to help kids mature and show us what they can do over a longer period of time. The environment needs to be more supportive and less structured to allow children to grow, and they all grow at different rates, especially at this time of their lives. Kids should start school when they are five years old, not within several months before or after their fifth birthday – a few months plus or minus to a little person who has only been on the planet a total sixty months is a long time in developmental terms. Class sizes need to be made much smaller for these reasons, and staffed by incredibly talented, and superbly trained teachers with adequate support staff to back up their efforts. To offer a class size number to discourse, I would not venture beyond twelve students at this level. To this end, if we are really serious about teaching kids a second language, we should start it in first grade. Kids' heads are open vats containing vast sponges to soak up gobs of information. By the time a kid reaches junior high school, the traditional time second language instruction begins, research shows that the part of the brain that receives it is closing itself up.

Special education requires a long, hard look. As an institution, it is failing miserably, and we are spending gobs of money on it. Research indicates that special education classes have a majority of boys. Worse, they are boys of color. Each district uses different guidelines to screen students for special education, and what qualifies a student for special education in one district does not qualify the student in another, even if the districts are next door to each other. Special education does not improve graduation rates. Its scope and sequence obviates the parent from responsibility to insuring what happens in school is followed up at home. If we can reduce the numbers of students assigned to special education, we can pay for smaller class sizes as mentioned above. There is a wide gap of what is defined as "learning disabled." It needs to be narrowed. With smaller classes, better-trained teachers, and more involved parents, students with special needs can be treated more fairly.

Do not give grades in grades six, seven, and eight. Rather, this time should be used to authentically reevaluate students for the high school, and should include intense parent-teacher conferences at least eight times per year. This is the last time we have for innovative intervention before kids start to train for careers or college, or both. We need to be sure we have done everything we can to help kids read and do mathematics through basic algebra and geometry. Courses in technology should be limited to creating critical problem-solving skills. Art should be used as a means to help students understand the breadth of their talents and gain their interpretations of their world through non-language means. All of this needs to be authentically evaluated and discussed. Plans for those students with shortcomings in math and reading need to be developed for continuation at the high school level, with the proviso that they be adapted as the student chooses a course of study. Rather than grades, take the time to have parent conferences six times a year.

Go to six marking periods. Most schools use four and send home nebulous progress reports that do not tell the real story as to how kids are doing. Keeping parents informed is the first step in keeping them involved.

There needs to be a formal connect between K-12 and higher education and industry. It must be fluid, collegial, and have the formal ear of the government. When the bodies that bring these three entities together call for recommendations of curricular or structural changes and are backed by broad-based research, they need to be acted on quickly by policy-makers.

Remember, kids don't vote. Therefore, they should be above politics, not ignored by it.

Occupational education needs to be revalued. That is, there are some courses that should be taught as on-the-job-training by craftsmen or practitioners, and others that need to be upgraded with the use of the latest technology. All of these courses should have industry internships and specific connections to community colleges, and in some instances, four-year colleges. Secondary schools dealing with specific technologies need to be created where students are immersed in subject-specific learning, while other programs have students for part of the day or part of the week. To this end, federal programs like Tech Prep and School-to-Careers need to be revisited and expanded. They worked.

Physical education needs to be changed in scope and sequence. We are a nation that is totally out of shape and bent on consuming fast food. A period of forty-five minutes three days a week is obviously not helping. A good deal of this time is spent in dressing and undressing into and out of gym clothes. Sports-for-life programs to accompany traditional sports programs need much more time to be effective. Perhaps, then, PE should be offered on a basis of extended time and extended expectations. Further, it should be opened up to the community at large. For this to happen, PE needs to be given over longer periods on the weekends, evenings, and early mornings, as well as during the school day if innovative scheduling permits. Specific physical goals and time spent need to be established for each student to meet, just as it would be if the student were to go to a fancy spa or private gym.

Like PE, home economics, technology, art, and a host of other courses should be open to adults and students at hours outside the regular school day, much like adult education courses are. More kids would take these courses if their class schedules could make room for them, but more times than not, the school day is crammed with courses. In the days of NCLB, where a third year of math and science is required in many states (something I insist is misguided), these courses are often precluded. However, if they were offered in the evening and on weekends for kids and community members, their ranks would swell.

Let's revisit local property taxes for a moment. While we are saddled with the present inequity of school funding, I suggest that individuals should only pay school tax increases while their kids are in school. When they graduate, they still should pay a flat rate for education, because education should be a community affair open to all who come to partake from its table for the nourishment of the mind, no matter what their ages.

It's wise to remember that when William Levitt built his first housing developments in the late 1940's and early 1950's, the homes were little more than 1100 square feet, and families of six individuals or more lived fairly comfortably in them. The behemoths that are built today are generally over 3600 square feet, and families are smaller. If you can afford this kind of house, don't complain about your school taxes. It's like walking into a Ferrari showroom and asking about gas mileage.

Study the extracurriculum. Examine how it succeeds, and then apply those lessons to the classroom. To this end, I would suggest that readers of this book witness the genius and spirit that arises by participation in the US First Robotics Competitions that begin each March. Talk to the teachers and kids about how it has changed their lives. We owe a debt of gratitude to its founder, Dean Kamen (who invented the Segway and a host of other high-tech products). He showed us kids can really think, and their teachers can easily support them if the environment is so disposed.

I dislike NCLB, but in all fairness, there are two accounts on which NCLB succeeded:

a.   It brought attention and money to education,
b.   It made education "sexy" enough to be a major part of political discourse.

It failed on three accounts:

c.   It is underfunded, and over managed far from the center of reform, the classroom,
d.   It is an education on the cheap that has created many more problems than it solved, to include making schools glaringly inequitable and ungainly to manage effectively.
e.   It is stifling genius on all fronts by demanding sameness.

We can do better for our kids, our country, and ourselves, no matter what our ages. You can never learn enough. Schools should be community ventures to champion learning as a life-long edu-prise.

Epilogue—
To The Kids

No, I didn't forget you...
Why do it?
That's the question kids have been asking since there were schools, and you and I are no different in that venue. When I was in high school, we were told that we needed to be well-educated to insure we wouldn't wake up with the Russian hammer-and-sickle flag flying from our school's flagpole, put there by Fidel Castro and Nikita Krushchev themselves. After that, we had to worry about the fact that if we didn't stop the communist Viet Cong and North Vietnam from taking over South Vietnam, the whole of Southeast Asia would succumb to communism. I never figured out how education would be involved, but then again, lots of things were said by government officials in the 1960's that didn't make sense. After them, the Japanese and Germans became our enemies again because they were out-producing us, and their kids were working harder than our kids, and the whole of our country would be a playground for German and Japanese businessmen. We worried about the Russians since World War II until we outspent and outsmarted them because we did education better than they did.

Today, the enemy is...well, while terrorists need to be destroyed, they haven't got a country with any resources to outright destroy us, though they try to strike fear into our hearts with their brutal tactics and their absolutely guiltless passion for murder. For the most part, we've run out of enemies. We're the only superpower left in the world. With that come problems. While we can out-gun anyone, we may not be able to out-smart them for too long, because there are so many of them doing education better than we are.

143

While we have no bellicose enemies (other than those who murder), there are other countries in the world that are moving forward with lots of innovative programs. Have you looked at the populations of China and India lately? Our industries are "outsourcing" work to these enormous, increasingly technological populations to save money. What's more, this outsourcing is hyperactive within our high-tech industries, once thought to be our own intellectual monopoly. Here is the critical point: While the Japanese have copied our genius and the Germans have been more industrious and demanding in their production to make better products, we have always been the world leader in intellectual capital. We invent things better than anybody. We have the greatest source of genius on the planet. This comes from the fact that we are a long-standing democracy of free thinkers, even though we are one of the youngest countries on earth. Democracy makes way for the individual to have unfettered off-the-wall ideas that have created thousands of ingenious machines, processes, thoughts, art, music, and technology. This is what the world is envious of. It's also where they want to surpass us. They want what we've got. It's not that they are outwardly greedy or seditious; they know what we've got works, and they want it to work for them like it works for us. We cannot fall behind. We need to keep up just so we can negotiate from a position of strength, not weakness. At the end of the day, it would be best if we all came away from the thought exchange as friends and had dinner together.

So why should you do it? It's simple, and really no different than why I basically did it, and those who preceded me—do it for yourself, and the kid in the next row. Do it for those who cannot do it for themselves.

Your standard of living will depend on how much you can keep ahead of the technology curve before someone else catches up. This is similar to the arms race of the later half of the last century, where engineers came up with bigger bombs, faster planes, and bigger tanks. Nonetheless, the mightiest weapon and the best product is a thought, not a cannon. It has always been that way, but now increasingly so. It's a different kind of war where the weapons kill no one, but simply eliminate their ability to earn a living. The casualties can be just as catastrophic.

While our educational system is not at all perfect, it's the only one we've got—for now. If we are ever to maintain our intellectual leadership, education needs to be better. I'm reminded in a book I read as a teenager that had a chapter dedicated to the outbreak of World War II and its affect on an aircraft carrier, the USS Enterprise, which finished the war as the nation's most decorated warship. The ship's antiaircraft guns needed replacing. Some of her aircraft were downright obsolete. Other aircraft had no self-sealing fuel tanks or armor plate, which meant they could be destroyed in fire or blood. The ship's fire extinguishing system needed updating. However, the author pointed out that war is fought initially with the weapons at hand. It would be wrong to think of the current educational state of affairs as a war, but it serves as a good metaphor. The schools we have right now, for all their imperfections, are all we have at hand. We need to make the best of them. You especially need to make the best of them.

In the meantime, clamor for change. Go to school board meetings. Visit your state, county, and town legislators, and ask them what they are thinking about and tell them what you are thinking about. Voice your concerns. You are children of the greatest democracy on earth. You are your country. Act like it. Be responsible to yourself and to each other, because in the long run, you are all you have got. Change your school through your extracurricular involvement. It is where you shine, and it is all yours. There are no state curricula as to how to run the West Coast Offense, the full court press, pitch a slider, perform in a play, the debate team, or math club. Your teachers are released from the curriculum and are more your mentors, and they evaluate you more authentically. Spend time thinking about you. Reflect on who you are, where you have come from, where you want to go, and how to make that happen. Don't drown in your present – you've got much more future than past or present, so place yourself there, and work on staying there. Be realistic in terms of covering all your bases. For example, no matter how athletically talented you may be, the chances of you playing in the NBA or NFL are slim to none. Nonetheless, continue to dream about it, because some of you will play in the NBA or NFL. However, work hard at developing the other dreams you will conjure up as your abilities and inabilities become clearer to you as you age. Don't put up with anyone or anything that gets in the way of your dreams. Seek alternatives and seek out those who can provide them. Don't hang with losers who see their lives bordered by the end of the block or the interstate.

More so, don't let the media tell you how to live your life. It is your life. You are directing, producing, and starring in it. You should not be an audience watching someone else live your life for you. This isn't a dress rehearsal—you get only one chance to get it right. You can stumble and fall, you can change course, and you still can succeed grandly. Just remember, you only get to do it once.

For this book, I met recently with members of what Tom Brokaw called The Greatest Generation, that group of people who fought off The Great Depression, fought and won a World War against forces darker and more evil as any in history, and then came back to peace to create the greatest economy the world has known. When I started to talk about you, one said, "Oh, my! I couldn't be a youngster today. Things are so unsafe." Another said, "Poor kids. They grow up without families. To us, families were everything. Who helps them?" Still another said, "They are all so much prettier and handsomer and stronger than we were. And smarter! I guess they validate us by doing so well." An octogenarian lady with sparkling blue eyes said, "They call us the greatest generation. I think they are. Their world is so much faster and hurtful. They have so much to worry about. Still, they smile and talk to us as we pass them by. They make us feel we still count." Another grizzled veteran of Omaha Beach pointed a crooked, arthritic-ridden index finger and said with authority, "I wish I had some of those kids soldiering in Iraq with me during my war." Not one of them criticized you or your culture. I, too, cannot heap enough praise on you for what you do. After watching kids for thirty-six years, I'm still amazed at what you have accomplished in such little time against so much adversity.

An admissions representative from Princeton University recently told me, "When I'm at a cocktail party and people start putting down kids, I remind them that the reason Princeton is so much more competitive than it was twenty years ago is because there are so many more talented kids!"

While it is up to adults (with input from you) to make schools better, a good deal rides upon your shoulders. No matter how perfect we make the process of education, you still have to do it. If you work at doing what you need to do, change may come much more swiftly than you think. If I may offer any criticism, it is that you do not appreciate how very good you are, or the possibilities you have. You look ahead. Your best teachers "got your back." To that end, I hope this book helps. Most importantly, have fun, and respect and take care of each other.

References

Advanced Placement Annual Report (2003). New York: The College Board.

Amrein, A.L. & Berliner, D.C. (2002). High stakes testing, uncertainty, and student learning. Educational Policy Analysis Archives, 10, (18). Retrieved March 28, 2002 from http://epaa.asu.edu/epaa/v10n18/.

Ancess, J. (2000). The reciprocal influence of teacher learning, teacher practice, school restructuring, and student learning outcomes. Teachers College Record, 102, (3), 390-419.

Angus, D. L. & Mirel, J.E. (1999). The failed promise of the American high school, 1890-1995. New York: Teachers College Press, Columbia University.

Barker, B.O. (1986). The advantages of small schools. ERIC Clearinghouse on Rural Education, ED 265988.

Barr. S. (1993). Looking at the learning record. Educational Leadership, 57, (5), 20-24.

Black, S. (1993). Real life 101. Executive Educator, 15, (12), 24-27.

Botstein, L. (1997). Jefferson's children. New York: Doubleday.

Bouton, T.A. (1991) Problem finding: A case study of the origins of reform policy in New York State. Unpublished doctoral dissertation, Hofstra University.

Boyd-Zaharias, J. (1999) Project STAR- The story of the Tennessee class-size study. American Education, 23, (2), 30-36.

Boyer, E. (1983). High school: A report on secondary education in America. New York; Harper and Row.

Bracey, G.W. (2000). The 10th Bracey report on the condition of public education. Phi Delta Kappan, 82, (2), 133-144.

Brady, M. (2000). The standards juggernaut. Phi Delta Kappan, 81, (9), 649-651.

Brennan, R.T., Kim, J., Wenz-Gross, M., & Siperstein, G. N. (2001). The relative equitability of high stakes testing versus assigned grades: an analysis of the Massachusetts Comprehensive Assessment System (MCAS). Harvard Educational Review, 71, (2), 173-216.

Brunner, D.D. (1994). Inquiry and reflection. Albany: State University of New York Press.

Callan, E. (1988). Autonomy and schooling. McGill-Queen's University Press.

Conley, D. (2003). Mixed messages—what state high school tests communicate about student readiness for college. Center for Educational Policy Research, University of Oregon.

Charmaz, K. (1991). Good days, bad days. New Jersey: Rutgers University Press.

Cohen, D.K. & Ball, D.L. (2001). Making change: Instruction and its improvement. Phi Delta Kappan, 83,(1), 73-77.

Conant, J.B. (1959). The American high school today. New York: McGraw-Hill.

Conant, J.B. (1967). The Comprehensive High School. New York: McGraw-Hill.

Cookson, P.W. (2003). Standardization and its unseen ironies— why testing is part of the dumbing down of America. Education Week, 22, 19, pp. 30-32.

Corbett, H.D. & Wilson, B.L. (1990). Unintended and unwelcome: The local impact of state testing. Paper presented at the Annual Meeting of the American Educational Research Association. Boston, MA (ERIC Document #377234).

Corsaro,, W.A. & Eder, D. (1990). Children's peer cultures. Annual Review of Sociology, 16, 197-220.

Cotton, K. (1996). Affective and social benefits of small-scale schooling. ERIC Clearinghouse on Rural Education and Small Schools. (EDO-RC-95-5, December, 1996).

Council of Chief State School Officers (2000). Key state education policies on K-12 education:2000. Washington, D.C.

Covington, M.V. (1996). The myth of intensification. Phi Delta Kappan, 25, (8), 24-26.

Cuban, L. (1990). Reforming again, again, and again. Educational Researcher, 19, (1), 3-14.

Cusick, P.A. (1973). Inside high school. New York: Holt, Rinehart & Winston, Inc.

Cummins, J. (1986). Empowering minority students: a framework for intervention. Harvard Educational Review, 56, 1, pp. 18-36.

Darling-Hammond, L. (1991). National goals and America 2000: Of carrots, sticks, and false assumptions. Education Digest, 57, (4), 5-28.

Darling-Hammond, L. (1994). Performance-based assessment and educational equity. Harvard Educational Review, 64, (1), 5-22.

Darling-Hammond, L. (1995). Restructuring schools for student success. Daedalus, 124, (4), 4-11.

Delpit, L.D. (1993). The silenced dialogue: power and pedagogy in education other people's children. In Wesi, L & Fine, M. (Eds.)

Beyond silenced voices—class, race and gender in United States schools. Albany: State University of New York Press.

Denzin, N.K. (1977). Childhood socialization. San Francisco: Jossey-Bass.

Deschenes, S., Tyack, D., Cuban, L. (2001). Mismatch: Historical perspectives on schools and students who don't fit them. Teachers College Record, 103, (4), 525-547.

Dewes, S. (1999). The School-within-a school model. (ERIC Clearinghouse on Rural and Small schools EDO-RC-99).

Dewey, J. (1916). Democracy and education. Toronto: The Free Press.

Dewey. J. (1916). How we think. In Fullan, M. (1982). The meaning of educational change. New York: Teachers College.

Dewey, J. (1916). My pedagogic creed. In J. Dewey, The early works, Vol. 5 (pp. 84-95). Carbondale: Southern Illinois University Press. (Original work published
in 1897).

Doolittle, G., Nablo, S., & Carbone, T.A. (1998). The big house. Educational Administration Quarterly, 34, (3), 380-396.

Dowd, J. (1990). Ever since Durkheim: the socialization of human development. Human Development, 33, 138-159.

Draper, A. (1906). Academic examinations and academic funds. An address at the 44th University Convocation of New York State.

Dworkin, G. et al. (1999). Elementary school retention and social promotion in Texas: An assessment of students who failed the reading section of the TAAS. Houston: Sociology of Texas Research Group—University of Houston.

Easton, L.B. (2002). Lessons from learners. Educational Leadership, 60, 1, pp. 64-69.

Eisner, E.W. (2000). What does it mean to say a school is doing well? Phi Delta Kappan. 82, (5), 367-372.

Ellmore, R.F.& Fuhrman, S.H. (2001). Holding schools accountable: Is it working? Phi Delta Kappan, 83, (1), 67-72.

Eisner, E.W. (2003). Questionable assumptions about schooling. Phi Beta Kappan, pp. 648-657).

Fine, M. (1991). Framing dropouts: Notes on the politics of an urban public high school. Albany: State University of New York Press.

Finn, C.E. & Petrilli, M.J. (Eds.) (2000). The state of state standards. Washington, D.C.: Thomas B. Fordham Foundation:

Finn, J.D. (1998). Class size and students at risk: what is known? What is next?
A Commissioned Paper, National Institute on the Education of Students at Risk, U.S. Department of Education.

Freire, P. (1998a).The adult literacy process as cultural action for freedom. Harvard Educational Review, 68, (4), 480-499.

Freire, P. (1998b). Politics and education. California: UCLA

Freire, P. (1998c). Pedagogy of Freedom. New York: Rowan & Littlefield, Inc.

Freire, P. (1998d). Cultural action and conscientization. Harvard Educational Review, 68, (4), 499-522..

Freire, A.M. & Macedo, D. (1998e).The Paolo Freire reader. New York: Continuum

Freire, P. (1997) Mentoring the mentor—a critical dialogue with Paolo Freire. New York: Peter Lang.

Freire, P. (1996). Letters to Cristina. New York: Routledge.

Freire, P. & Macedo, D. (1995). Dialogue: Culture, language, and race. Harvard Educational Review, 53, (3), 377- 403.

Freire, P. & Gadotti, M. (1995). We can reinvent the world. In Critical Theory in Educational Research, McLaren, P. L. & Giarelli, J.M. (Eds.) Albany: State University of New York Press.

Freire, P. (1993). Pedagogy of the city. New York: Continuum.

Freire, P. & Faundez, A. (1989). Learning to question. New York: Continuum.

Freire, P. (1974). Pedagogy of hope. New York: Continuum.

Freire, P. (1973). Education for critical consciousness. New York: Continuum

Freire, P. (1970). Pedagogy of the oppressed. New York: Seabury.

Fritzberg, G.J. (2000). Escaping the shadow of "excellence": A preview of my argument for revisiting equity concerns in the context of standards-based reform. Multicultural Education, 8, (1), 37-44.

Fullan, M. (1982).The meaning of educational change. New York: Teachers College Press.

Fullan, M.G. (1991). The new meaning of educational change. Cassel Educational: London.

Gardner, P.W., Ritblatt, S.N., & Beatty, J.R. (2000). Academic achievement and parental involvement as a function of high school size.The High School Journal, 83, (2), 21-27.

Gallagher, C. (1991) An ethnographic investigation into a re-medial secondary summer school. (Doctoral dissertation, Hofstra University, 1991).

Giroux, H. (1991). Educational leadership and the crisis of democratic culture. Paper presented at the UCEA Convention, University Park, PA. (ERIC Document Reproduction Services ED366086).

Giroux, H. (1988). Teachers as intellectuals. Massachusetts: Bertin & Garvey.

Giroux, H. & McLaren, P. (1986). Teacher education and the politics of engagement:The case for democratic schooling. Harvard Educational Review, 56, (3), 213-238.

Goodlad, J. (1984). A place called school. McGraw-Hill; New York.

Goodlad, J.I. (2003). A nation in wait. Education Week, V22, n32, April 23, 2003.

Goodman, J. (1989). Education for critical democracy. Journal of Education, 171, (2), 89-115.

Goldman, A. E., & McDonald, S.S. (1987). The group depth interview—principals and practices. New Jersey: Prentice-Hall.

Gordon, S.P. & Reese, M. (1997). High stakes testing; worth the price? Journal of School Leadership, 7, (4), 345-368.

Goals 2000: Educate America Act (1994). HR 1804. One Hundred Third Congress of The United States of America

Gould, S.J. (1981). The mismearsure of man. New York: W.W. Norton

Graff, G. (2003) Trickle Down Obfuscation . Education Week, v22, n9, June 4, 2003.

Gratz, D.B. (2000). High standards for whom? Phi Delta Kappa, 81, (9), 681-687.

Grissmer, D.W., Kirby, S.N., Berends, M., Williamson, S. (1994). Student achievement and the changing American Family. RAND Corporation. Available on the Internet— HYPERLINK http://www. http://www. uncg.edu/edu/ericass/achieve/docs/rand_cha.htm.

Gurwitsch, A. (1966). Studies in Phenomenology and Psychology. Evanston: Northwestern University Press.

Guskey, T.R. (1994). High stakes performance assessment-perspectives on Kentucky's educational reform. Thousand Oaks, CA.: Corwin Press.

Habermas, J. (1991). The theory of communicative action. Boston: Beacon Press.

Habermas, J. (1979). McCarthy, T. (ed.) Commuciative action and the evolution of society. (Boston: Beacon Press).

Hargreaves, A. (2001) Ed. Learning to change: Teaching beyond subjects and standards. San Francisco: Jossey-Bass Publishers.

Hargreaves, A. (2001). The knowledge society. Columbia Teachers College (In press).

Hatch, T. (2000). What does it take to break the mold? Rhetoric and reality in new American schools. Teachers College Record, 102, (3), 561-589.

Heubert, J.P. & Hauser, R.M., Eds. (1999). High Stakes: testing for tracking, promotion, and graduation. Washington, D.C.: National Academy Press.

Hodgkinson, H. in Goldberg, M.F. (2001). Demographics—ignore them at your peril. Phi Beta Kappan, 82, (4), 304-306.

Hoffman, L.M. (2002). What students need in the restructured high school. Education Week, 7, 7, pp. 34-38.

Holmes, C.T. (1989). Grade level retention effects: a meta-analysis of research studies. In Shepard, L.A. & Smith, M. L. (eds.) Flunking Grades. London: Falmer Press.

Honderich, T. (1995). The Oxford companion to philosophy. New York: Oxford University Press

Houston, P. (2000). Statement delivered to Congressional Education Committee, June 19, 2000, 2261 Rayburn HOB, Washington D.C.

Jacobson, L. (2001). Survey finds mixed views on smaller schools. Education Week, October 3, 2001.

James, A. & Prout, A. (1990). Constructing and reconstructing childhood: contemporary issues in the sociological study of childhood. London: Falmer Press

Jervis, K. & Montag, C. (1991). Progressive education for the 1990s: Transforming practice. New York: Teachers College Press

Johnson, K. & Ross, H. (2001). Teaching to higher standards–from managing to imagining the purposes of education. HYPERLINK www.TCRecord.org. www.TCRecord.org.

Jones, K. & Ongtookuk, P. (2002). Equity for Alaskan natives: can high stakes testing bridge the chasm between ideals and realities? Phi Delta Kappan, 83, (7), 499-503.

Jones, M.G., Jones, B.D., Harding, B. Chapman, L, Yarbrough, T., Davis, M. (1999) The impact of high stakes testing on teachers and students in North Carolina. Phi Delta Kappan, 81, (3), 199-203.

Kaufmann, P., Bradby, D., & Teitelbaum, P. (2000). High schools that work and whole school reform: raising academic achievement of vocational completers through the reform of school practice. (ERIC Document Reproduction Services #ED438418).

Klein, S.P., Hamilton, L.S., McCaffrey, D.F. & Stecher, B.M. (2000). What do test scores in Texas tell us? Education Policy Analysis Archives, (8), 1-26. On-line HYPERLINK WWW.epaa.asu.edu/epaa/v8, www.epaa.asu.edu/epaa/8, 49.

Kober, N. (2001). It takes more than testing: Closing the achievement gap. A Report of The Center on Education Policy, Washington, D.C.

Kohn, A. (1999). The schools our children deserve. Boston: Houghton-Mifflin.

Kohn, A. (2000). The case against standardized testing-raising the scores, ruining the schools. Portsmouth, New Hampshire: Heinemann.

Kohn, A. (2001). Fighting the tests: A practical guide to resucing our schools. Phi Delta Kappan, 82, (5), 349-357.

Koretz, D. M.. & Barron, S.I. (1998). The validity of gains in scores on the Kentucky instructional results information system. RAND Institute: Washington, D.C.

Kornhaber, M. L. & Orfield, G. (2001). Raising standards or raising barriers? Inequality of high stakes testing in public education. New York.: The Century Foundation Press.

Kozol, J. (1991) Savage inequalities. New York: Crown Publications.

Kunkel, R. C., Thompson, J.C., & McElhinney, J.H. (1973). School-related alienation: perceptions of secondary school students. Paper presented at the meeting of the American Educational Research Association 57th annual meeting, New Orleans, LA. (ERIC Document Reproduction Service No. 074092).

Lee, F.R. (2001) Tested. The New York Times, Sunday, November 11, 2001.

Lee, V. E. & Smith, J.B. (1995). Effects of high school restructuring and size on early gains in achievement and engagement. Sociology of Education, 68, (4), 129-152.

Lee, V.E. & Smith, J.B. (1997). High school size: which works best and for whom? Educational Evaluation and Policy Analysis, 19, (3), 201-227.

Lee, V.E., Smerdon, B.A., Alfeld-Liro, C. & Brown, S.L. (2000). Inside large and small high schools: curriculum and social relations. Educational Evaluation and Policy Analysis, 22,(2), 147-171.

Lee, V.E., Smith, B., & Croninger, R.G. (1995). Issues in restructuring schools. Issue Report No. 9., Center on Organization and Restructuring Schools. Available at HYPERLINK http://www.wcer. wisc.eduhttp://www.wcer.wisc.edu.

Levin, B (1995). Improving educational productivity through a focus on learners. International studies in educational administration. In Hargreaves, A. (1997) Rethinking educational change with heart and mind. Association for Curriculum and Development 1997 Yearbook.

Levin, B. (1999). What is educational administration anyway? Educational Administration Quarterly, 35, (4), 546-561.

Linn, R.L. (1994). Assessment-based reform: challenges to educational measurement. Position Paper for The Annual William H. Angoff Memorial Lecture, Princeton, NJ. ED 393875

Linn, R.L. (2000). Assessments and accountability. Educational Researcher, 20, (2), 4-14.

Lomax, R.G., West, M. M., Harmon, M.C., Viator, K.A., Madaus, G.F. (1995). The impact of mandated standardized testing on minority students. Journal of Negro Education, 64, (2), 171-185.

Luijpen,W.A. (1966). Phenomenology and humanism. Pittsburgh: Duquesne University Press.

Maehr, M.L.& Maehr, J.M. (1996). Schools aren't as good as they used to be; they never were. Educational Researcher, 25, (8), 21-24.

Suarez-Orozco, M. & Gardner, H. (2003). Educating Billy Wang for the world of tomorrow. Education Week, 23, 8, pp. 34-44.

Marzano, R. J. & Kendall, J.S. (1996). A comprehensive guide to designing standards-based districts, schools, and classrooms. Aurora, Colorado: Mid-continent Regional Educational Laboratory.

Mazzeo, C.J. (2001). Examining examinations: assessment policy in historical perspective. Doctoral Dissertation, Stanford University: Digital Dissertations Publication Number AAT 3000066.

Meisels, S.J. & Liaw, F. (1993). Failure in grade: Do retained students catch up?. Journal of Educational Research, 87,(2), 69-77.

Merchant, B. (1995) Current educational reform: Shape-shifting or genuine improvement in the quality of teaching and learning? Educational Theory, v45, n2, pp 1-18.

McCarthy, T. (1985) in Habermas J., Theory of communicative action. Boston: Beacon Press.

McCarthy,T. (1991). Systems theory: complexity and democracy. In Honneth, A. and Joas, H. (Eds.) Communciative action. Cambridge: MIT Press

McColskey,W. & McMunn, N. (2000). Strategies for dealing with high stakes state tests. Phi Delta Kappan, 82,(2), 115-120.

McLaren, P. (1989). Life in schools. NewYork : Longman.

McNeil, L. (1986). Contradictions of control: school structure and school knowledge. NY: Routledge & Kegan Paul.

McNeil, L. (2000). Contradictions of school reform: educational costs of standardized testing. New York: Routledge.

McNeil, L. (2000a). Creating new inequalities: contradictions of reform. Phi Delta Kappan, 81, (10), 729-724.

McNeil, L. & Valenzuela, A. (2001). The harmful impact of the TAAS system of testing in Texas: beneath the accountability rhetoric. In Orfield, G. & Kornhaber, M.L. (Eds.) Raising Standards or Raising Barriers, 127-150. New York: Century Foundation Press.

Meier, D. (1995). The power of their ideas: Lessons for America from a small school in Harlem. Boston: Beacon Press.

Meyer, R. H. (1996). In H.F. Ladd (Ed.) Holding schools accountable: performance-based reform in education (pp. 137-145). Washington, DC: the Brookings Institution.

Nathan, L. (2002). The human face of the high stakes testing story. Phi Delta Kappan, 83, 8, pp. 595-600.

National Association of College Admissions Counselors Annual Journal, (2003).

National Commission on Excellence in Education (1983). A nation at risk. Washington, D.C. U.S. Government Printing Office.

Nelson, J. (2000). Overview of student performance on the 2000 TAAS. Executive Bulletin, Texas Education Agency. Available on line at www.Texas Education Agency.edu

Neisser, U. (1986). The school achievement of minority children. New Jersey: Lawrence Erlbaum Associates.

Nieto, S. (1994). Lessons from students on creating a chance to dream. Harvard Educational Review, 64, (4), 492-496.

Oakes, J. (1985). Keeping track: how schools structure inequality. New Haven: Yale University Press.

Ogbu, J.U. (1978). Minority education and caste. New York: Academic Press.

Oldfather, P. (1995). Songs "come back most to them": students' experiences as researchers. Theory Into Practice, 34, 2, pp. 131-136.

Osterman, K. (2000). Students' need for belonging the school community. Review of Educational Research, 70, 3, pp. 323-367.

Oxley, D. (1994). Organizing schools into small units: Alternatives to homogeneous grouping. Phi Delta Kappan, 27, 7, 521-526.

Pasch, M., Kacanek, P., & Huyvaert, S. (1998). Follow-up study of the 1997 Pine Valley, Michigan high school graduating class. Research Report 143, Eastern Michigan University. (ERIC Document Reproduction Service No. ED 423 279).

Pasi, R. (2000). The SOL: no easy answers. Educational Leadership, 57, (5), 75-76.

Phelan, P., Locke Davidson, A., & Cao, H.T. (1992). Speaking up: student perspectives on school. Phi Delta Kappan, 73, (9), 698-704.

Piaget, J. (1974). Understanding causality. New York: W.W. Norton.

Piaget, J. (1973). To understand is to invent: the future of education. New York: Grossman.

Popham, W. J. (2000). The mismeasurement of educational quality. School Administrator, 57, (11), 6-9.

Porter, A. (2000). Doing high stakes assessment right. School Administrator, 57, 11,
28-31.

Ramirez, A., & McClanahan. R. (1992). Reporting to the public. The American School Board Journal, 25, 2, pp. 33-35.

Qvortrup, J., Bardy, J., Sgritta, G., & Wintersberger, H. (Eds.) Childhood matters- social theory, practice, and politics. Brookfield: Avebruy.

Ravitch, D. (1996). In Berger, J., Does top-down standards-based reform work? A review of the status of statewide standards-based reform. NASSP Bulletin, 84, 612, 57-65.

Ravitch, D. (Ed.) (2001). Introduction. Brookings Papers on Education Policy, 1-8. The Brookings Institution: Washington, D.C.

Raywid, M. (1996). Taking stock: The movement to create mini-schools, schools- within-schools, and other small schools. (New York: ERIC Clearinghouse on Urban Education).

Raywid, M. (1999). Current literature on small schools. (ERIC Clearinghouse on Urban Education EDORC 988).

Richardson, J.K. (2000). The impact of block scheduling on student performance on the Virginia Standards of Learning End-Of-course assessments. (Doctoral dissertation, The College of William and Mary, 2000). Digital Dissertations publication number AAT 9974941.

Ritchie, C.C. (1971). The eight-year study: Can we afford to ignore it? Educational Leadership, 12, (6), 484-486.

Roellke, C. (1996). Curriculum adequacy and quality in high schools enrolling fewer than 400 pupils (9-12). (ERIC Document # ED401090).

Rogers, M.F. (1983). Sociology, ethnomethodology, and experience—A phenomenological critique. Cambridge: Cambridge University Press.

Rotberg, I.C. (2001). A self-fulfilling prophecy. Phi Delta Kappan, 83, (2), 170-171.

Rudduck, J., Day, J., & Wallace, G. (1997). Student perspectives on school improvement. In the Association for Supervision an Curriculum Development 1997 Yearbook: Rethinking educational change with heart and mind, 73-89.

Sarason, S.B. (1997). What should we do about school reform? School Psychology Review, v26, n1, pp. 104-110.

Scheurich, J.J. & Skrla, L. (2001). Continuing the conversation on equity and accountability: Listening appreciatively, responding responsibly. Phi Delta Kappan, 83, (4), 322-326.

Scheurich, J.J., Skrla, L., Johnson, J.F. (2001). Thinking carefully about equity and accountability. Phi Delta Kappan, 82, (4), 293-299.

Schlechty, P. (2001). Inventing better schools: an action plan for educational reform.
San Francisco: Jossey-Bass

Seltzer, D. (1995). Connecting school improvement in Iowa: Establishing shared direction. Paper presented to the Ninth Connecting School Improvement Institute, Des Moinses, Iowa, November, 1995.

Senge, P. (1990). The fifth discipline. New York: Doubleday

Senge, P. (1995). In O'Neil, J. On schools as learning organizations:A conversation with Peter Senge. Educational Leadership, n9, v22,April 1995

Senge, P. (1999). The dance of change. New York: Doubleday Currency

Senge, P. (2000) Schools that learn. New York: Doubleday.

Shepard, L. A. (2000). The role of assessment in a learning culture. Educational Researcher, 29, 7, pp. 4-14.

Sipes, R.B. (2000). The not-so-secret formula for successful change. Principal, 80,

(3), 35-43.

Skrla, L. (2001a).The influence of state accountability on teacher expectations.The Review, 52, 2, pp. 1-4.

Smith, F. (2001). Just a matter of time. Phi Delta Kappan, 82, (8), 573-576.

Sobel, T., in Ohanian, S. (2001). News from the test resistance trail. Phi Delta Kappan, 82,(5), 363-366.

Spring, J. (1976). The great sorting machine—National educational policy since 1945.

New York: David McKay Company.

Steinberg, L. (1996) Beyond the classroom. Why school reform has failed. (ERIC Document Reproduction Services #ED398346).

Cookson, P.W. (2003). Standardization and its unseen ironies—why testing is part of the dumbing down of America. Education Week, 23, 19, pp. 30-32.

Sullivan, B.T. (1993). Economic ends and educational means at the White House:A case for citizenship and casuistry. Educational Theory, 43, 2, 109-121.

The College Board (2001) SAT highlights report for 2001.

Tucker, M.S. & Codding, J.B. (1998) Standards for our schools. San Francisco: Jossey-Bass.

Tucker, M.S. (1999) in Marsh, D.D. & Codding, J.B. The new American high school.Thousand Oaks: Corwin Press.

Tyack, D.B. (1967).Turning points in American educational history. Massachusetts: Blaisdell Publishing Company.

Valencia, R.R. (1993).The uses and abuses of educational testing: Chicanos as a case in point. ERIC Document reproduction services No. ED387 287).

Viadero, D. (2001). DOD-Run schools cited for closing achievement gap. Education Week, 21, 7, pp. 23-24.

Wagner, T. & Sconyers, N. (1996). "Seeing" the school reform elephant: connecting policy-makers, parents, practioners and students. (ERIC Document Reproduction Services # ED400078).

Waksler, F. C. (1991). Studying the social worlds of children. New York: Falmer Press.

Wasley, P.A.& Lear, R.J. (2001). Small schools, real gains. Educational Leadership, 58, (6), 22-27.

Wasserman, S.(2001). Quantum theory, the uncertainty principle, and the alchemy of standardized testing. Phi Beta Kappan, 83, 1, pp. 28-40.

White E. (1983). Poll finds public endorsement of school reforms. Education Week, August 31, 1983, 1-10.

Yankelovich, D. (2001) How can we stop managed care from happening to education? In Sheriday ,D (Ed.), College Board Review, 192, January-February

Young, R.E. (1990). A critical theory of education-Habermas and our children's future. New York: Teachers College Press.

Printed in the United States
46434LVS00004B/23

9 781932 172232